# 5 CITIES *That* RULED *the* WORLD

## DOUGLAS WILSON

**THOMAS NELSON**
*Since 1798*

NASHVILLE   DALLAS   MEXICO CITY   RIO DE JANEIRO   BEIJING

Published in Nashville, Tennessee, by Thomas Nelson. Thomas Nelson is a registered trademark of Thomas Nelson, Inc.

Page design: Mike McDaniel

Thomas Nelson, Inc., titles may be purchased in bulk for educational, business, fund-raising, or sales promotional use. For information, please e-mail SpecialMarkets@ThomasNelson.com.

Scripture quotations noted ESV are from THE ENGLISH STANDARD VERSION. Copyright © 2001 by Crossway Bibles, a division of Good News Publishers.

Scripture quotations noted NEB are from THE NEW ENGLISH BIBLE. Copyright © 1961, 1970 by The Delegates of the Oxford University Press and the Syndics of the Cambridge University Press. Reprinted by permission.

**Library of Congress Cataloging-in-Publication Data**

Wilson, Douglas, 1953-
    Five cities that ruled the world : how Jerusalem, Athens, Rome, London, and New York shaped global history / Douglas Wilson.
        p. cm.
    Includes bibliographical references and index.
    ISBN 978-1-59555-136-8
    1. Civilization, Western--History. 2. World history. 3. Cities and towns—History. I. Title.
    CB245.W554 2009
    909—dc22

                                                                2009031680

*Printed in the United States of America*

09 10 11 12 13  RRD  6 5 4 3 2 1

This book is for my father, Jim Wilson.
He loves this kind of stuff.

CONTENTS

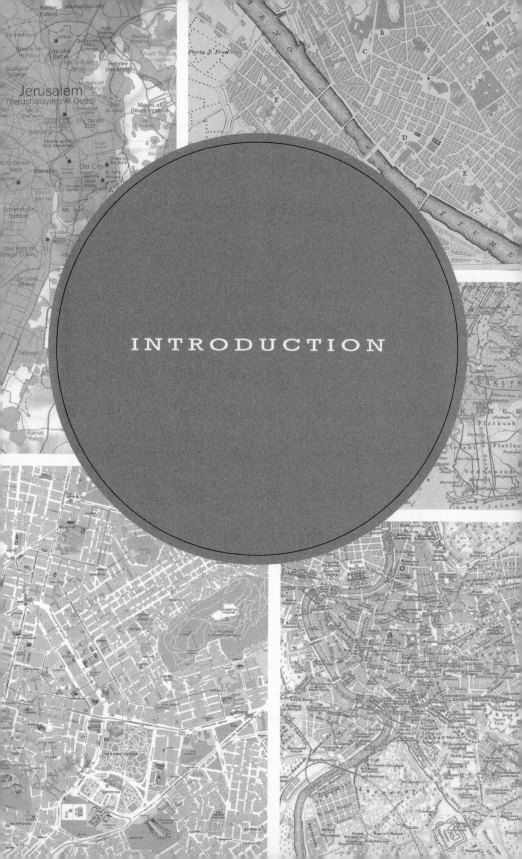

# INTRODUCTION

Jacques Ellul, a French theologian and writer, once noted the intertwined nature of human history and the city: "All of man's history is not limited to the history of the city and its progress. But they have nevertheless intermingled, and neither can be understood alone."[1] Here we will be considering the stories and legacies of the great cities of Jerusalem, Athens, Rome, London, and New York and what they mean to us.

They ruled the world in a unique way, unlike other cities. No earthly city can rule the world forever, but many more than five have ruled the political world temporarily. These five have been singled out because, despite their moments of glory shared with many others, they have also had an enormous influence down to the present day. In many ways that influence is more potent than the power of triremes (ships with three levels or banks of oarsmen) or rockets.

As Scripture tells the story of the world, it begins with a garden, and it ends that story with a Garden City. Social critic David Hegeman described the arc of this particular story very well: "Culturative history is God's unfolding purpose for man, in which mankind plays a chief role in the development and transformation of the earth from garden-paradise to the glorious city of God."[2] But in between these two visions, here in the murk of history where *we* live, we have a great deal of turmoil and difficulty, and a lot of that difficulty relates to the question, whatever are we to do about our cities?

Jacques Ellul took a pretty grim view of the situation: "The city is the direct consequence of Cain's murderous act and of his refusal to accept God's protection. Cain has built a city. For God's Eden, he substitutes his own."[3] On this take, the first thing that Cain wanted to do in his rebellion against God was to build a city. For Ellul, this was far more significant than Cain simply needing a way of getting the garbage collected and the mail delivered; it was a statement of fundamental religious rebellion. His city—named Enoch after his son—was established to compete with the God he had rejected.

At the other end of the spectrum from Ellul, we have the writers of travel guides. We have civic pride and hard-core allegiance to the sports teams of the nearest regional city. We have swelling patriotism, full of the kind of hope that wants us to see "alabaster cities gleam undimmed by human tears." We have poets, apparently a bit more realistic, who celebrate their particular city's prowess or accomplishments in a more earthy and clear-eyed fashion. Take Carl Sandburg's famous poem about Chicago,[4] for instance:

Hog Butcher for the World,
Tool Maker, Stacker of Wheat,
Player with Railroads and the Nation's Freight
    Handler;
Stormy, husky, brawling,
City of the Big Shoulders

Sandburg saw the problems that Ellul would identify as wickedness, and he even agreed that his city was wicked and bare-knuckled and crooked and brutal. But he gave the sneer back to the critic and celebrated his city anyway—"proud to be alive and coarse and strong and cunning." Perhaps this is what we should expect. As Jane Austen had Edmund say in *Mansfield Park*, "We do not look in great cities for our best morality." But even this may be illusory. I was once visiting my grandmother's home in a tiny, sleepy farm town in Nebraska. While there I saw a bumper sticker that said, "You don't see much in a small town, but what you hear makes up for it."

Even with such pressing problems, we shall see that Ellul's strictures are perhaps too severe. He pointed to an important truth, but we must not take it as the entire truth. There is another city besides Babylon, and each of these five cities (and all the others like them) has a relationship to this second city as well. If all cities are Babylon in one sense, what is the relationship of all cities to the New Jerusalem? After all, in the vision of this heavenly city that the apostle John was given, the kings of the earth bring their considerable honor *into* it: "By its light will the nations walk, and the kings of the earth will bring their glory into it" (Rev. 21:24 ESV). Not only do we have a *city* here, but we have all the rulers of all other cities paying their respects and submitting themselves to this glorious city. If all cities are wicked Babylon, what are they doing in here, inside the pearly gates?

The longer we work on such a thorny problem, the more necessary it will be for us as moderns to reflect on what previous generations have said about it. This *is* a perennial problem. If we are willing to hear Augustine on the subject, we will learn that ultimately there are only two cities—the City of God and the city of man. He wrote his great work of theological history, *The City of God*, in order to comfort Roman Christians who had been distressed by the sack of Rome—one of the cities we will be discussing shortly. After Constantine had made the Christian faith the faith of the empire, it had been easy for Christians to assume that the "Eternal City" had the future all sewn up. Rome ruled the world, and Christ was now the ruler of Rome. What could go wrong? So when a bunch of unwashed barbarians sacked the city, the psychic damage was far more significant than the actual physical damage done to Rome. How was this even *possible*? Augustine wrote this majestic work to teach these believers to distinguish the city of man from the City of God. If Rome is to be identified with the kingdom of God, then what happens to our faith when Rome falls?

So this is something that we clearly need to do, but the devil, as someone once said, is in the details. The boundary lines between the two cities are sometimes blurry—at least to us here in these twenty-first-century seats. As I have noted, Augustine worked on this problem with his description of the two cities. Martin Luther did something similar in his view of the "two kingdoms." The Puritans of New England sought to hammer out a closer working relationship between the two cities in their one "city on a hill." The problem has historically been a hard one within Christendom, and on either side of the faithful now is the option of radical Islam, where there is no such distinction between the cities, or secular liberalism, where the only city that matters is the city of man. In this latter view, one can believe in the City of God, if he likes, behind his eyes and between his ears, just as he can also believe in Farley's ghost.

A big part of the problem is the tension between faith and power. Civil governments rest upon force, and the gospel does not. How can these two principles ever abide together? There are some who have wanted the church to train its sons in the arts of politics, encouraging them to have their try at shinnying up the greasy pole of civic ambition. Others want the church to keep its prophetic purity, standing off at a distance, speaking truth to power. But as this history will show, from time to time, as it happens, power sometimes listens. What does the prophet do then? Theologian Peter Leithart asked, "To keep her integrity, must the Church *refuse* to succeed?"[5] Jonah went outside the powerful city of Nineveh, the city that had been spared through *listening* to him, and sulked about it.

At the same time, power *does* need to be spoken to. And some of the truths that need to be spoken are kind of obvious. Shelley's brilliant taunt[6] is one that all rulers of all great cities should have been made to memorize when they were little boys:

> My name is Ozymandias, King of Kings,
> Look on my Works, ye Mighty, and despair!
> Nothing beside remains. Round the decay
> Of that colossal Wreck, boundless and bare
> The lone and level sands stretch far away.

Nebuchadnezzar would have profited significantly from that exercise. The prophet Daniel warned him not to exalt himself in the way that rulers of great cities like to do. But he did not listen to the warning:

> All this came upon King Nebuchadnezzar. At the end of twelve months he was walking on the roof of the royal palace of Babylon, and the king answered and said, "Is not this great Babylon, which I have built by my mighty power as a royal residence and for the glory of my majesty?" While the words were still in the king's mouth, there fell a voice from heaven, "O King Nebuchadnezzar, to you it is spoken: The kingdom has departed from you, and you shall be driven from among men, and your dwelling shall be with the beasts of the field. And you shall be made to eat grass like an ox, and seven periods of time shall pass over you, until you know that the Most High rules the kingdom of men and gives it to whom he will." (Dan. 4:28–32 ESV)

It is very easy for people to assume that the way things are this minute will necessarily dictate the future. Historian John Glubb commented on this peculiar shortsightedness: "The people of the great nations of the past seem normally to have imagined that their pre-eminence would last forever. Rome appeared to its citizens to be destined to be for all time the mistress of the world. . . . Seventy years ago, many people in Britain believed that the empire would last forever."[7]

What follows is a popular history, but like all history, it is a matter of selection. Why these cities? Why this incident? Why this king? Why this year or that year? The historical writer, whether he is an amateur or a professional, is the one who does the selecting. It has sometimes been assumed that an accurate and objective history is one that simply records *all* the salient facts, as though video footage recording all events from sky cameras were somehow available at the university media center. There was a time when impressive historians embarked on this task with all the confidence of writers who knew that in *their* day gods walked the earth. But once it was realized, more recently, that all histories are selections made by that finite creature called the historian, the opposite mistake was easy to fall into. A frequent assumption in these postmodern times is that the whole enterprise is hopelessly subjective, and so one man's history is as good as another's. What works for you? In contrast to both these extremes, I want to remember a few basic principles before we visit our five cities.

*Cities are objects in the world that can be known.* Nothing close to omniscience is possible for any finite writer, but accuracy, honesty, and fair-mindedness are possible. I wrote these stories with a desire to tell the simple truth. While we don't know what we don't know, this does not lead us into relativism. Our knowledge is not exhaustive, but it can be accurate as far as it goes.

We have to remember that all that we do *not* know about the past is still present in some sense; the unknown past is still rushing beneath our feet. A. N. Wilson, in his short history of London, compared it to the Fleet River, which used to run above ground but is now underneath modern London. As he put it, "The history is there, hidden like the lost rivers, but in all effective senses it has been obliterated by what London in the last half century has done to itself."[8]

*Cities, like the men and women who live in them, have life spans, and that life span is approximately 250 years.* John Glubb pointed to this seemingly obvious truth, but one that is still routinely missed: "Any regime which attains great wealth and power seems with remarkable regularity to decay and fall apart in some ten generations."[9] When we are talking about a *great* city, we are usually talking about one that was the driving force in the establishment of an empire. Whether we are talking about the greatness of Athens, the authority of Rome, or the heyday of London, we are consistently dealing with roughly the same number of years. We should view the contemporary cities that share the name and occupy the same spot of land as their illustrious ancestors as civic grandchildren (modern London) or great-great-great-great-grandchildren (modern Rome).

So in regard to a city's life span, it would be more strictly accurate to say that a city's period of greatness has a life span. Cities are constantly changing and at some point the changes amount to a fundamental change. It makes sense to say that the Rome of Augustus is the same Rome as the Rome of Caligula. But we have stretched it past the breaking point if we try to include the Rome of Leo X. In the same way, the Jerusalem of David and the Jerusalem of Solomon are the same great city. But the Jerusalem besieged by crusaders is not, at least not in that same way. Each city is being included in large part because of what was done and accomplished during its time of greatness, but in larger part because of how that greatness has lingered and continued.

*Cities are moral agents.* They have an organic unity, and in that capacity it is possible (and necessary) to praise or blame them. The life span of a city's greatness is characterized by risk, courage, and sacrifice at the beginning, and by luxury and self-indulgence at the end. And when a prophetic voice addresses a city on the skids, the generalization does not mean there is no remaining virtue—just as there was obviously wickedness present during the time of the city's rise.

*Cities are loved by their sons and daughters.* This leads to the nettlesome problem of patriotism. Affection and love for your own people are an extended function of honoring your father and mother. When patriotism goes to seed, becoming a jingoistic nationalism, it gives patriotism a bad name. It is the difference between gratitude and arrogant pride. Patriotism stifles the spirit of war; nationalism breeds wars. Patriotism is catholic; nationalism is sectarian. Patriotism understands and enters into the affection that others have for their place.

Songs and poems reflect this deep love and affection that people will always have for their *place*—whether it is the sidewalks of New York, Virgil's poetic anticipation of Rome through the person of Aeneas, or Isaiah's ancient lament over Jerusalem. Love of place can certainly become idolatrous, and often has, but when this happens, it is because a natural human love has been wrongly elevated. We cannot hope to understand the influence of cities like Jerusalem, Athens, Rome, London, and New York without understanding how much they have been beloved. Great cities have been simultaneously respected and despised by those under their domination, but cities like these never rise to prominence without being loved by their citizens.

*Cities are the world.* The stories of representative cities cannot be told without involving the entire history of the world. Every discussion of past history brings with it certain assumptions about the trajectory of history overall, and this would have to include the future. Some assume that history meanders, more or less as it has always done. Others assume that history is locked in an inevitable decline. Still others (less common these days) have a deep faith that there is such a thing as actual progress, and that we have much to look forward to. As we discuss these cities—their past glories, their present influence, and their future—my assumption is that progress is real and genuine, and that we do have much to look forward to, not only in these five cities, but in all the places from which we may visit them.

What is the legacy of each of our five cities? Obviously, we are talking about many millions of people and scores of centuries. It is not possible to reduce the legacy of each city to one thing. But we can summarize, and we *can* generalize. Jerusalem has bequeathed to us a legacy of the spirit; Athens, reason and the mind; Rome, law; London, literature; and New York, industry and commerce. I hasten to add that these are not watertight categories. We cannot detach law from reason, the mind from the spirit, or literature from commerce. All these cities were founded and populated by human beings. In different ways, all of them represent all of us. Untangling what that means is the task in front of us.

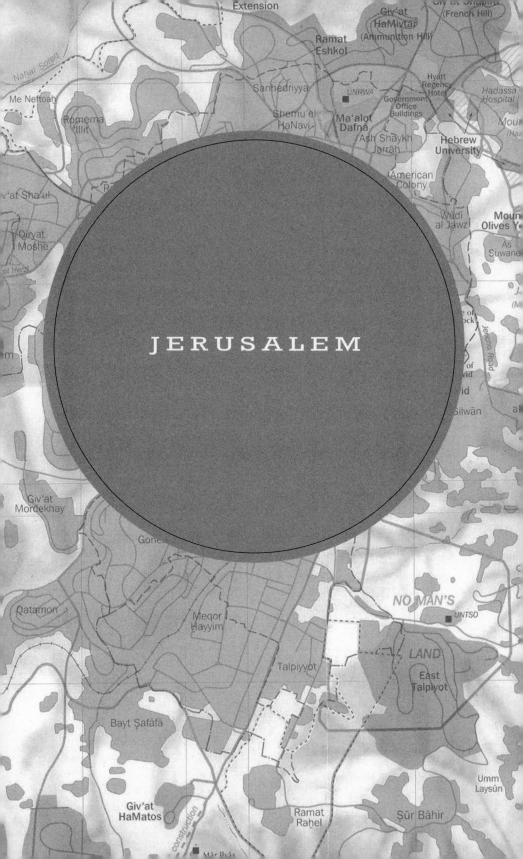

For many thousands of years, Jerusalem has been situated at one of the busiest intersections of history. From the wars of King David to yesterday's terrorist attacks, Jerusalem has consistently been in the middle of things. Today it is a holy city for three major religions, and that has been no small part of many of our current conflicts. In years past, because Jerusalem was situated in a perilous spot between major powers—whether those powers were Egypt, Babylon, Persia, Rome, or the Parthians—many armies met to fight there. So *that* caused significant problems. As a result, the city has known many masters—first the tribe of Melchizedek (unless he was a Jebusite), followed by the Jebusites, the nation of Israel under David, the Babylonians, the Persians, the Greeks, independence under the Hasmoneans, the pagan Romans, the Byzantine Christians, the Persians again for a few years, the Muslims, the crusaders, the Muslims again, the British, and an independent government of Israel in 1948, with the recapture of Jerusalem by the Jews in 1967. And I have probably left out some important lords-of-the-place-for-the-time-being, and I offer them my sincere apologies.

Jerusalem, the city of peace, has been a busy place of seemingly unending conflict. Pastor and educator George Grant quoted an observer who shrewdly noted that the constant strife in Jerusalem is not an interruption of its historical charm—that *is* Jerusalem's historical charm.[1] Despite this conflict (and some could argue because of it), the city has left us a legacy that does not depend on armies, a legacy of the spirit.

## Moriah and Melchizedek

Centuries ago, an elderly man named Abraham and his young son named Isaac were walking slowly toward the future site of Jerusalem. Servants accompanied them, but when they got close to the mountain, the father instructed the servants to stay where they were. He said that he and his son were going up on the mountain to worship God, and then *both* of them would return. That was a remarkable statement, given what the father planned to do on that mountain: take his son and sacrifice him there.

God had promised Abraham a lineage, but He had promised it specifically through Isaac. When Isaac was finally born to his aged parents, Sarah and Abraham, God tested Abraham. God instructed Abraham to "go to the land of Moriah, and offer [Isaac] there as a burnt offering on one of the mountains of which I shall tell you" (Gen. 22:2 ESV).

This story is often read as though it were a test of Abraham's love or dedication to God. But it was actually a test of *faith*. God had told Abraham specifically that he would have innumerable descendants and that they would be reckoned *through Isaac*. The test was whether Abraham was really going to believe God's promise.

This fascinating and terrifying story fits into our history of Jerusalem because of *where* Abraham's near sacrifice of Isaac occurred. At the end of the previous chapter of Genesis, Abraham was in Beersheba, which is a little less than fifty miles from the region of Moriah, where God had told him to go. And when he got there, God said that He would identify a *particular* mountain for Abraham. On foot, that's a long journey for one donkey and four men. Centuries later, the children of Israel were told that God would choose to set His name in a particular city (Deut. 12:5). King David accomplished that final settlement when he took the city away from the Jebusites, but the process of selection began with Abraham's wrenching journey to that place.

Men lived in this place long before the Israelites did, and the name goes back that far as well. The place was called *Uru-Salem* in ancient cuneiform tablets that have been discovered. *Uru* is related to an ancient word for city, and *Salem* was the name of a local god. But Salem is also close to the Hebrew word for peace—*shalom*—and so they thought of it as Jeru-shalom, the city of peace. Malchizedek, an ancient priest-king who lived there in the time of Abraham—several thousand years before Christ—was "king of Salem, that is, king of peace" (Heb. 7:2 ESV).

## David and Solomon

In the time of Abraham and Melchizedek, the Hebrews were a very small nomadic tribe. When Abraham's grandson Jacob went to live in Egypt, the band was around seventy or so. But when Moses led the people out of slavery a few centuries later, they had grown to a multitude—more than a million people. After the Israelites left Egypt and invaded Canaan from the east, from across the Jordan River, they were not able to conquer the land all at once. One obvious example was Jerusalem, inhabited by Jebusites, who were fairly certain of their prospects for defense. The Jebusites were a Canaanitic tribe, and all through the period of Israel's judges they were able to hold out against the Israelites. Their city was a natural fortress with a readily available supply of water. The time of the judges ended with the reign of Saul, who was followed by David, the second king over all twelve tribes. When David finally made the strategic decision to mount an assault on Jerusalem, the defenders were pretty cocky about David's chances. The Jebusites declared to him: "'You will not come in here, but the blind and the lame will ward you off'—thinking, 'David cannot come in here'" (2 Sam. 5:6 ESV).

Up to that point, the settlement of Canaan had been according to the allotment given to the various tribes. Abraham, Isaac, and Jacob were the patriarchs of Israel, and the twelve tribes were descended from Jacob's sons. The rise of David to power was part of a strong governmental consolidation, one that set the stage for a move away from tribal government. Once the city was in his hands, he made Jerusalem the "City of David," and it became a true capital city under his oversight.

David's son Solomon completed this task, dividing Israel into administrative provinces. Each district under Solomon had to provide the food for the palace for a month, which was no small burden. This centralization and increased taxation were "tolerable" because of the widespread prosperity, which is the way it frequently goes. David had anticipated this move because he had minimized the importance of tribal boundaries.

The ark of the covenant was the central embodiment of

God's presence with Israel, normally housed in the tabernacle's holiest place. When the time of the judges came to a disastrous end, Israel lost the ark to the Philistines in battle. After the ark of the covenant was recovered from the Philistines a short time later, David eventually had it brought back to Jerusalem. He established a tabernacle for the ark on Mount Zion, but no ongoing sacrifices were performed there.[2] It was a place for the sacrifices of praise and *music.* David was a notable musician, and this particular reformation introduced music into the worship of God, where it has since remained.

A generation later, when Solomon built the temple on Mount Moriah, the functions of David's tabernacle were moved to the temple, and the name Zion went along with those functions. From that time, the name Zion has been evocative. Not only did the name Zion move from Mount Zion to Mount Moriah, but by extension it also became another name for the entire city of Jerusalem.

A tantalizing historical possibility comes to us from this period. Could the Jerusalem of this era have been a key player in the exploration of the wider world? As Solomon consolidated his position on this land bridge between Asia and Africa, he gained control of a town called Ezion-geber, located on the Gulf of Aqabah. It gave Israel access to the Indian Ocean, away to the south and east. Solomon was not slow to make a treaty with the Phoenicians, a seagoing people, but a people who had no real access to the waterways of the east—where there was a great deal of water. The Phoenician city Tyre was to the northwest of Israel, and their ships were limited to the Mediterranean, and from there to the Atlantic. But Solomon built a fleet of ships at Ezion-geber in concert with the Phoenicians, and they began bringing gold back from a mysterious place called Ophir (1 Kings 9:26–28). The round trip took three years to complete (1 Kings 10:22). The phrase "ships of Tarshish" could be translated as "refinery ships," ships equipped to carry smelted ore. Although it may be a controversial suggestion to some, it is quite possible that the land of Ophir was Central America.

One of modern man's besetting sins is that of underestimating the capacities of ancient men. We do this sometimes even when faced with the evidence. The Phoenicians understood the arts of navigation well, and they had sailed remarkable distances. They had tin mines as far north as Norway, and they circumnavigated Africa by 600 BC or so. Yes, an objector might say, that they were just coastal hopping. We have no evidence that ancient men knew how to navigate across oceans, the objection continues, particularly an enormous ocean like the Pacific.

But consider this argument objectively. When modern man finally figured out how to navigate across oceans (hooray for us!), and when Captain Cook first reached the Hawaiian Islands, what did he find there? Well, he found *people*. It appears that *some* ancient men with rudimentary technology knew how to sail across the Pacific; otherwise, they wouldn't have done it. They didn't float out there on coconuts.

And when Cortez began his march across Mexico, what did he encounter? Massive civilizations, that's what. Moreover, the cultures and civilizations appeared to have quite a bit in common with the ancient civilizations of the Middle East. Those similarities would include architectural features like ziggurats and a high level of technical ability.

The Phoenicians had made it to New England across the Atlantic.[3] It is possible that they gave Solomon the expertise to establish staging areas across Polynesia and then mining colonies in Central America. If so, that was the main source of Solomon's fabulous wealth. The lines of communication with these colonies broke down later, with a later king of Judah named Jehoshaphat attempting to reestablish them, but unsuccessfully, and so the stranded colonists had to fend for themselves until the arrival of the Spanish.

We should banish from our minds all the quaint superstitions that we have heard about ancient men—that they believed the earth was flat, and other such nonsense. Ancient men knew the earth was a globe; they had calculated (with a fair degree of accuracy) the size of that globe. They knew that people lived on the other side of the globe (calling that region the *Antipodes*, which means their feet were sticking the opposite way ours do) and they had done a fair amount of exploring this globe. Never forget the evidence that tells us people inhabited the *entire world*—long before Columbus, long before Leif Eriksson, and long before St. Brendan, God bless them all.

If we may be allowed this harmless speculation, it places Jerusalem in a significant role in world history—a leader in settling their New World about two thousand years before it was *our* New World.

## EXILE AND RETURN

During the period of the judges before Saul and David, the twelve tribes of Israel had shared a common culture and (for the most part) a common worship, but they were radically de-centralized in their political structure. Ruled by various judges in various parts of the country, on what appears to have been a pretty ad hoc basis, they first came together in a united monarchy under Saul. His dynasty never really made it past him, though his son Ishbosheth managed to rule over part of Israel for a few years. The next king over all twelve tribes was David, and the third and *last* king of the united monarchy was David's son Solomon. Having three kings was a pretty short run.

When the United States was first being established and the Constitution was being debated, the men who wrote the Federalist Papers (urging adoption of the Constitution) were well aware of the regional strains and tensions that were already present between North and South. War did not erupt until the middle of the next century, but foresighted men could already see the trouble brewing. A similar tension was present throughout the course of the united monarchy of Israel, and when the split happened, it happened along the fault line.

The ten northern tribes broke off and formed their own nation, and Jeroboam, their first king, decided to establish distinct forms of worship for them. His reasoning was that if his subjects had to go to Jerusalem three times a year in order to worship God (which the law of Moses required), their allegiance would be perpetually divided—they would have civil loyalties to the North and religious loyalties to the South. And so he established centers of worship in the North for the North, at Dan and Bethel.

The Northern Kingdom of Israel was carried away into exile by Assyria in 721 BC. This event has led to many assumptions about "the ten lost tribes of Israel," along with theories that claim to have found them again. Yet these ten tribes were not really lost. Their national structure was lost, and unlike that of the Southern Kingdom, it was never recovered. Tribal identity is not the same thing. We have every reason to believe that numerous Israelites continued to be faithful to Yahweh, the covenant God of Israel, and that they continued to worship in the South. Elijah was told there were still seven thousand who had not bowed the knee to Baal. And because of the enormous pressure to submit to Baal worship, it is likely that a number of these faithful Israelites had moved south to Judah.

Seven centuries after the Assyrians took the ten tribes away, the apostle Paul could still refer to "our twelve tribes" (Acts 26:7 ESV). Anna the prophetess, who greeted Joseph and Mary at the temple, was of the tribe of Asher (Luke 2:36), one of the northern tribes. The Southern Kingdom consisted of Judah and Benjamin, and Levi supplied the priests for temple worship. So four of the twelve were mentioned by name, and the others included generally. The real problem with tribal identity did not occur until AD 70 when the temple was destroyed along with all the official genealogical records that were housed there.

After the Assyrian zenith, the Babylonians took their place as that region's superpower, and so Babylon destroyed the city of Jerusalem in 586 BC. Nebuchadnezzar conquered Jerusalem and the Jews were taken (in waves) into exile. Jeremiah had prophesied that the exile would be seventy years in length, but the waves going into exile, along with the waves coming out of exile, make the start and stop times difficult to pinpoint.

The simplest way to state the problem is to ask whether

Ezra and Nehemiah were contemporaries or whether they lived in back-to-back generations. For our purposes here, I am assuming that Ezra and Nehemiah lived at the same time. This means I am assuming that the same rulers are sometimes referred to by different names. A common practice in ancient times was the use of throne names. We see this readily in other circumstances. If someone today were to refer to Caesar, a natural question would be, "Which one?" The same is true of "Pharaoh."

One thing we should grant is the very real possibility that *Darius* and *Artaxerxes* were throne names. Other throne names in the Bible would be *Ben-Hadad* (Jer. 49:27; Amos 1:4) and *Abimelech* (Gen. 20; 26; Ps. 34). So an assumption in using the short chronology is that the shift from Darius to Artaxerxes in Ezra 7 does *not* represent the reign of a different king, but a change in the name used for him.[4]

The pagan kings overseeing the return were Persian, but we will use the Greek names for them: *Cyrus* (539–530), *Cambyses II* (530–522), *Darius I* (522–487), *Xerxes I* (487–466), and *Artaxerxes Longimanus* (465–425). The period involved stretches from 539 to 425 BC, and a glance elsewhere shows us that it was a busy time. The Greeks defeated the Persians at Marathon and Salamis, Pericles ruled in Athens, the Greek tragedians flourished, Socrates taught, Cincinnatus was dictator in Rome, and the Buddha and Confucius both lived and died.

My operating assumption here as I deal with the chronology of these books is that the Persian kings named Darius, Ahasuerus, and Artaxerxes in the books of Ezra, Nehemiah, and

Esther are the same man. I am assuming that all of it happened in the reign of Darius. This makes Ezra and Nehemiah, the men who rebuilt Jerusalem after the exile, contemporaries.

As we consider all this, understand that students of this subject differ and the confusion about these identifications is ancient, even going back to Josephus and apocryphal books. At the same time, the short chronology (assuming that Ezra and Nehemiah were contemporaries) does appear to be assumed in the books themselves. Ezra is mentioned in Nehemiah, for example (12:36), and Nehemiah is mentioned in Ezra (2:1–2; see also Nehemiah 7:7).

Unless the writer is trying to confuse us, we should assume that a different Nehemiah would be identified as such (as happened in Nehemiah 3:16). And in Ezra 2:2, Mordecai is mentioned. Why would this not be the great Mordecai of Esther 10:3? How many Jews would have this Persian name (which meant "man of Marduk")? What it amounts to is that we need to decide between a view that sees the same king with different names or a view that sees different men with the same name. And this latter option does not seem tenable when we try to see a different Ezra labeled as *Ezra the scribe*.

## FACING JERUSALEM

In this story of Jerusalem, what should we make of those Jews who were forcibly taken *away* from Jerusalem? For example, Daniel was taken into captivity under Nebuchadnezzar, but he was influential in Babylon for many years, down to the reign of Darius the Persian. Nevertheless, Daniel was always a citizen of

Jerusalem, oriented to the city in ruins. He prayed facing Jerusalem. And the resettlement of Jerusalem was very much on his mind. Having read the words of Jeremiah, he knew exactly how long the Exile had to be: seventy years (Dan. 9:2).

Just as Jews in Brooklyn and in America overall are extremely concerned about the fate of Jerusalem today, so were the Jews in Babylon during the Exile. They might not have been there physically, but their hearts were very much there. And because of that concern, the city was successfully rebuilt. This is, in microcosm, the kind of influence that Jerusalem has exerted throughout most of its history.

Now, if the chronology I am using is correct, Mordecai was part of the contingent of Jews returning to rebuild Jerusalem. This would also mean that Esther was the queen. After Esther had replaced Vashti as queen, Mordecai overheard a plot on the king's life and told her about it (Est. 2:19–23). At just that moment, it happened that Mordecai refused to bow down before Haman, who as a result plotted to kill all the Jews (3:1–15). But it is not likely that Haman was flying off the handle here—there was a backstory that takes us to the land of Jerusalem. When the book of Esther opens, Haman and Mordecai were already looking coldly at each other across the saloon, right hands twitching just above their holsters. Haman was an Agagite, a descendant of the Canaanite Agag, the king of the Amalekites, the king whom Samuel executed when Saul failed to. And Mordecai was a descendant of Kish, Saul's father, a shirttail relative of the man who had neglected to kill Agag.

When Haman manipulated the king into signing a decree against the Jews, Mordecai persuaded Esther to make an appeal to the king (4:1–17). She did so, and as a result of her shrewd intervention, Haman was eventually hanged (7:1–10). The king sent out a second edict, allowing the Jews to defend themselves (8:1–17), and the Jews took this opportunity to defeat and kill their enemies (9:1–19). To honor the victory, the holiday of Purim was established (9:20–32). The story ended with Mordecai being promoted (10:1–3). That enabled him to return to Jerusalem—in honor and not in disgrace.

And so this is how the story of Esther is facing Jerusalem, like all faithful Jews in exile. She was probably sitting right there when Nehemiah made his famous request to the king to rebuild the city (Neh. 2:6). At the heart of the story of Esther, we find the rise of Mordecai, and he was among those who returned to Jerusalem. Jerusalem is one of the cities that rule the world because of its gravitational pull on people who no longer live there. That remains the case today, and it was the case in the first exile of the Jews from their homeland.

## HASMONEANS

Under the leadership of Nehemiah and Ezra, the city walls and the temple were rebuilt. All this occurred while the Persians were in power. But as the Persians expanded to the west, they encountered stubborn resistance from scattered city-states in Greece. I will tell that story more fully in the chapter on Athens, but I do need to note here the broad outlines of what happened.

The Greeks stopped the westward expansion of the Persian Empire at the battle at Marathon and the battle of Salamis. Athens assumed supremacy among the Greek city-states and had a moment of glory. But a short time later, internal fighting sapped the military strength of the Athenian confederation and the less-sophisticated Greeks in Macedonia to the north came into their own. Philip of Macedon consolidated their power, and then his son, Alexander, took the show on the road. He swept through all the nations to the east, up to the border of India. He wanted to conquer more, but his troops did not really want to visit lovely Japan and drew the line.

As it happened, Alexander died in Babylon on the way home. That entire part of the world was then under Hellenistic influence, but without Alexander it was not possible to hold it all together in a unified empire. Hellenistic culture was planted everywhere, but the political situation was fragmented. Two of the fragments were the Ptolemaic dynasty in Egypt, which was Hellenistic, and the Seleucid dynasty in the area of Syria and beyond, also Hellenistic. Per the usual game plan, Jerusalem happened to be in the zone of conflict between them.

When Alexander had charged through that region before— to bring Jerusalem under his authority—he had not sacked the city as most expected he would. The high priest had come out to meet him and, according to Josephus, Alexander saw "the high priest in purple and scarlet clothing, . . . he approached by himself . . . and had given the high priest his right hand . . . he came into the city; and when he went up into the temple, he offered sacrifice to God, according to the high priest's direction, and magnificently treated both the high priest and the priests."[5]

Alexander did this because he had had a dream back in Macedonia, when he was thinking about how to overthrow Persia, and in that dream a man dressed just like the high priest exhorted him to cross the sea and conquer the Persians. After the sacrifice in Jerusalem, the Jews brought out their Scriptures. Josephus described what happened next: "When the book of Daniel was showed him, wherein Daniel declared that one of the Greeks should destroy the empire of the Persians, he supposed that himself was the person intended; and as he was then glad, he dismissed the multitude for the present."[6]

Although Alexander did not destroy the city of Jerusalem, and though he conquered Persia in accordance with the prophet Daniel, the legacy he left was a legacy of conflict for Jerusalem. That legacy included two kinds of conflict. One, just mentioned, was the conflict between rival Greek factions after Alexander's death. The other was the conflict between Hellenistic culture and Jewish culture.

Both were real problems. Fashionable Greek influence became pervasive among the Jews. A gymnasium in the Greek style was built in Jerusalem near the temple, and faithful Jews began to see their traditions and customs eroding, sometimes quite drastically. An example of the former would be the behavior of Antiochus IV, king of the Seleucids, who thought to eradicate Judaism. Pigs were to be sacrificed in the temple to Greek gods. Daniel had warned about this ruler, calling his actions the abomination of desolation. Many examples of the former were the means of filling up the room with explosive fumes. The decision of Antiochus to make war on faithful Jews was the spark: "On his return from the conquest of Egypt, in the year [169 BC], Antiochus marched with a strong force against Israel and Jerusalem. In his arrogance he entered the temple and carried off the golden altar, the lamp-stand with all its equipment . . . and took them all with him when he left for his own country" (1 Macc. 1:20–24 NEB). Not content with insulting their religion, the king then declared that the Jews must abandon it.

About the only thing missing from this scenario is that he didn't do all this in the name of diversity, the way it would be done today. The penalty for resisting his decree was death.

The revolt was led by a priestly family, the Hasmoneans, beginning with Mattathias. He killed a Jew who was about to offer a compromised sacrifice, and then he killed the officer presiding over the affair. He and his sons took to the hills and began to wage a campaign against the Gentiles. After Mattathias died, the guerrilla campaign was taken over by his son Judas Maccabeus. He fought so ably that he liberated Jerusalem and cleansed and rededicated the temple, profaned as it had been by Antiochus.

> They celebrated the rededication of the altar for eight days; there was great rejoicing as they brought burnt-offerings and sacrificed peace-offerings and thank-offerings. . . . There was great merry-making among the people, and the disgrace brought on them by the Gentiles was removed. Then Judas, his brothers, and the whole congregation of Israel decreed that the rededication of the altar should be observed with joy and gladness at the same season each year, for eight days. (1 Macc. 4:56–59 NEB)

This was the basis for celebrating Hanukkah, the Feast of Lights. Although it is not one of the feasts required by the law of Moses (as with Purim, established in the book of Esther), the celebration has taken deep root among Jews.

The men who established this brief period of independence for the Jews were clearly great and wise men, but the same thing cannot be said for all their descendants. Once the Hasmonean family became established rulers in Israel, a similar thing happened to them that happens to many rulers. About a century later, two brothers from this family got into a dispute over who should be on the throne, and it was not an example of, "No, really, *you* should have it."

In 63 BC, these two descendants of the Hasmonean line asked Rome—in what must have seemed like a good idea at the time—to arbitrate the dispute. When the Hasmoneans refused the results of the arbitration, the Roman general Pompey took advantage of the situation and easily took over. The brief independence of Israel was snuffed out, and the land became a Roman client state. Pompey tried to rule through Hasmoneans at first, but that didn't work too well. In 37 BC, Herod the Great came to the throne.

## HEROD AND THE SECOND TEMPLE

Before we talk about Herod and his tenure, a little math problem needs to be cleared up. Solomon built the first temple, which was destroyed by Nebuchadnezzar. The second temple was built in the time of Ezra and Nehemiah. But some of the older men who remembered Solomon's temple wept because (even though the dimensions were the same) the glory of the first far surpassed the glory of the second. But by Herod's era, the temple was magnificent, and scholars refer to this period among the Jews as *Second* Temple Judaism.

Actually, the temple built in the time of Ezra and the temple Herod built were the same temple—*kind* of. Rabbi and historian Abraham Millgram described the process that Herod used:

> In building the Temple, Herod was scrupulously careful not to violate the religious sensitivities of the people. In order not to defile the sanctity of the existing Temple, the builders within were recruited exclusively from among the priests, and in order not to interrupt the Temple ritual, the new structure was erected over the old one. Only when the new Temple was completed was the old building dismantled and removed from within.[7]

Herod was the grandson of an Idumean (an Edomite, meaning that he traced his lineage from Esau and not Jacob) who had converted to Judaism. His father had been an important functionary in the court of the last Hasmonean king, and it appears that in terms of ritual observance, Herod was fully Jewish. He wanted very much to be accepted by the Jews as a legitimate king, but the Jews largely regarded him as a lickspittle to the Romans. Part of the reason he had trouble getting the Jews to recognize and accept him as their king lay in the fact that he was a cruel, paranoid man. Herod's personality was revealed fully when he was unsettled by the story of the wise men and decided to kill all baby boys in the area of

Bethlehem. That kind of action will drive your poll numbers down every time.

At the same time, the Jews were extremely proud of the temple that Herod provided for them. The temple complex took up about one-sixth of Jerusalem's available area, covering about thirty-five acres. It was placed on the very summit of Mount Moriah, facing the east and the Mount of Olives. The temple was plated with gold, and according to Josephus, it was not possible to look at it directly when the sun was shining on it. It was an *impressive* structure.

Today the few remnants of the temple complex (such as the Wailing Wall) are actually stones in retaining walls to make a level place for the temple to stand and were not part of the temple itself. The temple took forty-six years to build (John 2:20), and before another forty had passed, it was destroyed.

Herod the Great died in 4 BC, and since he was the one who attempted to take the life of the infant Jesus, we can conclude that our dating systems of BC and AD are slightly out of kilter. The system was not instituted until centuries after the birth of Jesus, and it represented the best guess of that time. Readjusting everything now would really mess things up. But a Scythian monk named Dionysus, who went to Rome around AD 500, made the proposal for a new calendar. Historian and theologian N. T. Wright described his work this way: "Of course, he got it wrong, and so shall we. Considering the material available to him, he did a pretty good job of working out Year 1 of the new era; but we now know that Jesus of Nazareth was almost certainly born in what he, and we, call 4 BC."[8]

At any rate, the New Testament regards the time in which

Jesus lived as the century in which the old order of sacrifices at the temple was abolished, as the decisive moment at the hinge of the history. Dionysus made a proposal to help us recognize this fact centuries afterward, but there was a strong awareness even in those days that momentous things were afoot.

After Christ's resurrection, His followers scattered everywhere, preaching the gospel of a new era of salvation for humanity. Sometimes they were helped to scatter by persecutions, and other times they were driven by missionary zeal. As a result of their proclamation, Gentiles began to stream into the church, and the first great controversy to afflict the church was settled at the Council of Jerusalem (Acts 15). The question before the house was whether Gentiles were allowed to become Christians without becoming Jews first. The question was settled in favor of the position urged by the apostle Paul, and a new kind of person was established. No longer would Jew and Gentile have to fight with each other—God was making one new man out of the two (Eph. 2:15). It was not long before these people were called *Christians*; that happened first at Antioch (Acts 11:26).

According to Christians, the sacrificial system of the Jews was fulfilled and superseded by the sacrificial death of Christ on the cross. And if the sacrifices were superseded, what need was there for a temple? A temple was a place for sacrifices. That is why, from the earliest years, the Christians had begun to think in terms of a spiritual Jerusalem, a heavenly Jerusalem. The Jews represented the old guard, wanting to keep the temple establishment operating. But as it happened, the catastrophic events of the first century overtook them all, just as Jesus had predicted.

Jesus began His ministry when He was around thirty. He

was born in 4 BC, so that puts the beginning of His ministry at or around AD 26. We know that His ministry extended over at least three Passovers; this brings us to AD 29 or 30. At the end of His life, Jesus predicted that Jerusalem was going to be destroyed. Expectation of the fulfillment of that prophecy pervades the New Testament. Some of the language used is so vivid that a number of Christians have taken it as a description of the end of the world, but Jesus was primarily referring to the end of the Judaic eon. He said that it was all going to happen within a generation, which in the Bible is reckoned at forty years. And that was what happened—on the dot.

The revolt against Rome broke out in AD 66. According to Josephus, more than a million people died during the siege at Jerusalem. Although the tensions frequently ran high between Jewish Christians and non-Christian Jews before this, the destruction of Jerusalem put the seal on it. The Christians fled for Pella across the Jordan, which was precisely the kind of thing Jesus had said to do when they saw Jerusalem surrounded by armies (Luke 21:20–21). But the other Jews regarded their flight as a betrayal and desertion. The Christians, for their part, saw the destruction of Jerusalem as God's judgment on the Jewish people for rejecting Jesus as their Messiah.

The war was begun, on the Roman side, by Vespasian. His son Titus completed the final conquest of Jerusalem. When the conflict first exploded, an impartial observer might have thought that the Jews had a good chance of success. Vespasian did not complete the siege because Rome was racked by civil war, and he had to return home in order to take over as emperor. Nero was forced to commit suicide and was followed by three emperors in quick succession (each one ruling mere months) until Vespasian came home from Jerusalem to put everything into good order.

In addition, the Jews were tenacious fighters and they had a preeminently defensible city. Students of history debate whether it was right or wrong to use the atomic bomb on Japan in the Second World War. But in the midst of that debate, one of the most remarkable things sometimes overlooked is that it took *two* of those bombs to bring Japan to the point of surrender. Something similar happened with the ancient Jews. The Romans devastated Jerusalem in AD 70, but a little more than fifty years later, they had to do it *again*.

A charismatic fighter named Bar Kokhba headed the second revolt. The Romans had not treated the Jews gently after the first destruction, and in AD 132, the second revolt erupted in fury. It took the Romans three full years to put down the revolt, and hundreds of thousands of people died in the conflict. The last battle in that revolt was at Betar, and the Jews were finally defeated on the ninth day of Av. Ironically, it was the anniversary of the destruction of the first temple in 586 BC, as well as the date for the destruction of Herod's temple in AD 70.

By then the Romans were in no mood to fool around, and the Jews were exiled from Jerusalem permanently. Abraham Millgram noted that "Roman power prevailed; Jerusalem was not only sacked, but its very name was erased from the map. The Romans plowed over the city and built in its place a pagan city named *Aelia Capitolina*. No Jew was permitted to enter let alone reside in the new Roman city."[9]

In the phase of history that followed, Jerusalem was not a

strategic *political* spot. After Roman power became Christian, and the Roman center shifted east and became Byzantine, the capital of Palestine was Caesarea—under Christian rule. When the Muslims had ruled there, Ramle was the seat of government and Gaza was the choice of the Mamelukes (also Muslim). But despite this, Jerusalem remained a holy place for Christians, Muslims, and Jews, and thus it was a bone of contention in the centuries to come.

## MUSLIM ERA

Muhammad, a native of Mecca, was born around AD 570. When he was twelve, his uncle took him to Syria, where a Nestorian Christian monk prophesied over him. At the age of twenty-five, he married his first wife, Khadija, in a ceremony performed by an Ebionite Christian priest—a cousin of his wife. Fifteen years later, he began receiving his first "revelations" from the angel Gabriel. He was at first worried that they were signs of demonic possession, but his wife assured him they were from God. Three years later, he began to preach openly in Mecca about the revelations, but most of his peers rejected him and his words.

Finally, thirteen years after his first revelations, he fled from Mecca to Medina. This flight, called the *hijira*, marks "year one" of the Muslim calendar. His first wife had died, and at that point many of the distinctive features of Islam took shape, most notably the demand for complete submission. He married the daughter of one of his most loyal followers (a girl named Aisha, six years old), consummating that marriage when she was nine.

Later he took on other wives. He became a marauder and pirate, ordering attacks on Meccan caravans. Two years later, Muhammad ordered assassinations in order to gain control of Medina, and in AD 630 he conquered Mecca. Tribes from all over that area submitted to his authority. He died of a fever just a few years later, around the age of sixty-three.

Before he died, Muhammad sent out letters to many world leaders, demanding their submission; and in the years following his death, the Islamic faith exploded out of the Arabian peninsula. Jerusalem fell to Muslim conquerors in AD 638.

The Muslim era of expansion was just beginning, however. The high-water mark of the first Muslim expansion ended in France just shy of one hundred years later, at the battle of Tours (or Poitiers) in 732. A king named Charles Martel turned back what had been, up to that time, an apparently invincible force. Islam made it to India in the east and to France in the west. The Mediterranean had become a Muslim lake. As one person put it, if the Nobel Prize committee had been active in the year 1000, all the prizes would have gone to Muslims.

The next period of attempted Muslim expansion into Europe was centuries later. The Ottoman Turks were defeated in the great siege of Malta (1565) and the sea battle of Lepanto (1571), and they were finally turned back from the walls of Vienna in 1683 (ironically, fought on September 11–12). But Jerusalem, from virtually the beginning of the Muslim expansion, was under the authority of the "house of Islam."

This situation set the stage for many of our modern conflicts. If we go by the adage that possession is nine-tenths of the law, and we note all the groups that have had possession of

Jerusalem (and this goes even if we limit it to extant groups that at some time have had possession of Jerusalem for centuries), we still have a tangle of competing claims.

Matters are not helped when we recognize the antipathy between some of these groups, an antipathy that is not limited to ownership of Jerusalem. To understand this, we have to realize that the holy book of the Muslims, the Koran, is organized not chronologically but by length. This leads many people to think that the "peace" verses and the "war" verses in the Koran are all jumbled together, to be sorted out by Islamic theologians as the occasion demands. But the peace verses were from Muhammad's first Meccan period, when he was initially trying to persuade Jews and Christians, and they were subsequently *abrogated* by the jihad verses that began in Medina, when Muhammad turned to the sword.

As we will see shortly, Christian forms of non-Zionism need not be anti-Semitic, and for believing Christians, it must not be. But Muslim opposition to Jews and Israel is virulently anti-Semitic, and unfortunately, this attitude is grounded in the Koran. So long as the Koran is considered to be the word of Allah, this aspect of the problem cannot be solved. The final (and binding) revelation given to Muhammad about Jews (and Christians) was this: "Make war on them until idolatry shall cease and God's religion shall reign supreme" (Surah 8:39).

The difficulty for fundamentalist Muslims is that the need for warlike violence toward Christians and Jews is grounded in their sacred text, while at the same time success on the battlefield has eluded them for centuries. In the early centuries, they were on a roll and their theology matched what was actually happening. But since the siege of Malta, the battle of Lepanto, the siege of Vienna, and down into our century, they have had a theology *of* violence that has been consistently bested *at* violence.

At the battle of Lepanto, to take one example, the opening rounds from the new Christian gunships devastated the Muslim fleet. Military historian Victor Davis Hanson put it this way: "Most of the Christian observers believed that a third of the Ottoman armada was scattered, disabled, or sunk before the battle proper between galleys had even commenced."[10] The same kind of pattern has continued to the present. The outbreak of nonconventional violence in modern politics (terrorism) has to be seen as a sign not of militant strength but of a deep and profound frustration.

## THE CRUSADES

We are taught to speak of the crusades as an unmitigated evil, like the Holocaust or thousands of human sacrifices in a row at an Aztec temple. In Christian apologetics, a standard objection that an evangelist must learn to handle is, "What about the crusades?" Let it be said at the outset, there *is* quite a bit to apologize for. In 1095, when Pope Urban II launched the First Crusade, crusaders massacred thousands of Jewish residents in Europe in order to get into fighting trim. The problems didn't stop there. Even a (comparative) defender of the crusades like historian Serge Trifkovic insisted on acknowledging this:

What the Crusaders did to the Muslim inhabitants of Jerusalem in 1099 was as bad as what the Muslims had done to countless Christian cities before and after that time, but the carnage was less pardonable because, unlike the Muslims, it was not justifiable by Christian religious tenets. From the distance of almost a millennium, however, it is time to see the phenomenon as Christendom's reaction to Muslim aggression.[11]

The Seljuk Turks had captured Jerusalem. Although the previous rulers in Jerusalem were also Muslim, they had allowed Christian pilgrims and Christian worship. But under the Seljuk Turks, various atrocities were committed that inflamed Christians everywhere. The Seljuk Turks pillaged and murdered; they desecrated holy places. And something in Europe popped. After Islam had exploded out of Arabia in the seventh century, Muslims had put Europe in a defensive posture completely for three centuries. The Muslims had not overrun Europe entirely, but *it was not exactly because of a lack of trying*. When this new state of affairs blew up in the Holy Land, Europe was finally ready to fight back in a serious way. Trifkovic stated, "The Crusades were a belated military response of Christian Europe to over three centuries of Muslim aggression against Christian lands, the systemic mistreatment of the indigenous Christian population of those lands, and harassment of Christian pilgrims."[12]

But even when we regain a more accurate and balanced historical perspective, we have to acknowledge the atrocities on the Christian side. When this sort of thing erupts, the Bible does not encourage us to recognize the defense of, "Well, *they* started it." The Muslims did start it, and they had been militarily provocative for centuries. There is a fine case to be made that the crusades met the historic criteria of a just war. But Christian just war theory goes a step beyond this. From Augustine on, Christians have recognized the distinction between *jus ad bellum* (just cause in going to war) and *jus in bello* (just behavior in the course of fighting). This is the difference between having a just cause and pursuing that just cause in a just and worthy manner. On numerous occasions the crusaders failed to meet the second standard.

And so when the Christians finally fought back, they did not always fight clean or with the purest motives. Many were motivated by sincere piety, but others were keeping an eye on the main chance, others were running from the law, and others were seeking adventure. There were a few problems in how the fighters were urged on as well: "There was more than just a whiff of Muhammad in the papal guarantee of plenary absolution—a direct pass to heaven to the Crusaders should they die, or great riches if they lived."[13]

Be that as it may, the First Crusade was successful as measured by recapturing Jerusalem and making it available again to Christian pilgrims. After a siege lasting a little more than a month, the defenders surrendered. And under the leadership of Godfrey of Bouillon, the crusaders slaughtered tens of thousands of the inhabitants—both Muslims and Jews. Afterward, the Christian barons leading the army washed and changed their robes, and went to worship at the Church of the Holy Sepulchre. The dead were then buried, and the city was cleaned up and turned into a Christian city. The Al-Aqsa mosque was turned into a church, and the Dome of the Rock was transformed to Christian use.

But there was another problem. Remember that this was the eleventh century and a lot was going on in the world. William the Conqueror had taken England from the Anglo-Saxons in 1066, and shortly before that (1054) the Great Schism had severed the Eastern church from the Western church. There was one patriarch in the West, the bishop of Rome, while there were four patriarchs in the East—Alexandria, Constantinople, Antioch, and Jerusalem. The crusaders were Roman Catholics from the Western church, and when the patriarch of Jerusalem, who was Greek Orthodox, chose a time shortly before these events to die, the Latin crusaders responded by appointing Daimbert, archbishop of Pisa, to be the new patriarch of Jerusalem. Thus it was that the Latin Westerners alienated the local Christian population.

When the fighting was over, many crusaders wanted to return home. Keeping an army intact was a constant problem. After Godfrey died, his brother Baldwin replaced him. Baldwin reigned in Jerusalem from 1100 to 1118 and fought constantly with inadequate forces. He even resorted to drafting Christian pilgrims into his army.

This period also saw the rise of a new phenomenon in the West, which was that of the military monk. Those men were dedicated to making sure pilgrims could travel safely to the Holy Land. They had taken vows of obedience, chastity, and poverty. The best known of these orders was the Knights Templar, whose name came from where the founders lived, on the Temple Mount. Their residence was called *Templum Domini* and they took their name from this.

A bit earlier, another order founded in Jerusalem was

associated with the Hospital of St. John. It began as an order dedicated to helping sick and ailing people, and its members were called Hospitallers; over time they became an order of war-riors as well. What began as a defensive posture—escorting pilgrims—turned these orders that provided defense into the center of a standing army dedicated to perpetual war with Islam. The Hospitallers are best known for their magnificent defense of the island of Malta five centuries later against Suleiman, and they are now called the Knights of Malta.

But in historical terms, this Christian possession of Jerusalem was very brief. And after it relapsed into Muslim control, in the center of the Muslim world, the city did not play a major role until the beginning of the modern era.

## JERUSALEM TODAY

Tension in the Middle East today, centered in Jerusalem, is the result of two major developments. The first was the gradual eclipse of Islamic power, becoming undeniable and irreversible by the nineteenth century. The second was the rise of Zionism, or Jewish nationalism.

Historian Bernard Lewis described the decline of Islam:

For many centuries, the world of Islam was in the fore-front of human civilization and achievement. . . . And then, suddenly, the relationship changed. Even before the Renaissance, Europeans were beginning to make sig-nificant progress in the civilized arts. With the advent of the New Learning, they advanced by leaps and bounds, leaving the scientific and technological and eventually the cultural heritage of the Islamic world far behind them. The Muslims for a long time remained unaware of this.[14]

Jerusalem is the third holiest city for Muslims, surpassed only by Medina and Mecca. It is a city they ruled, in one fashion or other, for more than a thousand years. There were a few brief interruptions by the crusaders, barely measured in decades, but by and large the city was theirs. There had been earlier signs of trouble in the rise of Europe. The siege of Malta had gone badly for Suleiman in the sixteenth century, and the sea battle of Lepanto hadn't been pretty either. But by the nineteenth century, the complacency of the Ottoman Turks was shattered forever when it became evident that the Christian infidels could pretty much come or go in the Middle East at will.

Zionism accelerated after the Second World War and the Holocaust, but it was by no means created by either event. The father of modern Zionism—Theodor Herzl—was motivated by the trial of Captain Alfred Dreyfus, a French officer falsely accused of treason in 1894. But the obvious rise in anti-Semitism was not lost on Herzl, and he determined that the Jews needed a homeland of their own. The first Zionist Congress met in Basle in 1897, and the goal of Zionism was defined. "Zionism aims to create a publicly secured and legally assured home for the Jewish people in Palestine."[15] That phrase "in Palestine" is critical—the British had offered the Zionists a homeland in Uganda, which they declined. Zionism meant a homeland in Palestine, not just a homeland somewhere.

The establishment of the modern state of Israel is a fascinating story, but not a smooth one. Jerusalem was still under the Turks, but in the tangled politics surrounding the First World War, Britain endorsed the Zionist cause. That came in the form of the Balfour Declaration in 1917. Lord Arthur James Balfour was the British foreign secretary, and he stated the British intent in a letter to Lord Walter Rothschild: "His Majesty's Government view with favor the establishment in Palestine of a national home for the Jewish people, and will use their best endeavors to facilitate the achievement of this object."[16] That same year, General Sir Edmund Allenby bloodlessly captured Jerusalem from the Turks, ending their four-hundred-year stint there. Just a few years later, the League of Nations gave the Mandate of Palestine to the British government, and the declaration by Lord Balfour was in the official charter.

The situation on the ground was complicated from the beginning. Jews began coming to the city in significant numbers, Arab hostility to their presence became pronounced, and the British officials in Palestine tended in the main to be pro-Arab and anti-Zionist. Anti-Zionism is *not* to be equated with anti-Semitism (many ultraorthodox Jews in Jerusalem are anti-Zionist to this day), but it put the local officials at odds with the stated policy of their government. Just think of a conservative U.S. president trying to work something out by means of the liberals in the State Department and you have some idea of the picture. The Arabs were hostile and violent, the British officials were trying to accommodate them, and this in turn led to the rise of Zionist militancy, extremism, and some terrorism.

The British finally left in disgust in 1948, and Israel was declared a nation. At the same time, war erupted between the new Israeli establishment and the surrounding Arab neighbors. The immediate consequence of the war was that Jerusalem was divided into two sections—one controlled by Jordan and the other by Israel. Jerusalem was unhappily divided in this way until 1967, when Egypt, Syria, and Jordan launched an unprovoked war on Israel and were defeated badly. The most significant outcome from that war was that Jerusalem became a unified city again, under the control of Israel. And since Israel has had control of the city and all the holy sites, the Israelis have done remarkably well in allowing Christian and Muslim (and, of course, Jewish) pilgrims to visit their respective shrines and holy places.

So Zionism was the doctrine that resulted in the establishment of the modern nation of Israel. You have perhaps heard surrounding nations (like Iran) refer to Israel only as "the Zionist entity." But we have moved well past the point where Zionism is relevant anymore. You do not have to think nineteenth-century Zionism was a great idea to be willing to acknowledge that Israel's presence there *now* is an accomplished fact. Another doctrine functioning in the United States in the nineteenth century provides a helpful analogy. Manifest Destiny was the idea that the United States was destined to settle this country from the Atlantic to the Pacific. One hundred years after the fact, someone can believe that Manifest Destiny was a pernicious doctrine and yet live in Oregon or Nevada.

The reason the Jewish homeland had to be in Palestine was

ultimately theological. Although many leaders of the Zionist movement were secular and Israel is a secular state, Zionism caught fire in the Jewish imagination because Palestine was their ancient homeland. The capital city of Israel today is Jerusalem, just as it was for King David. Uganda wouldn't have served that purpose. For centuries Jews have reminded themselves of their exile from Jerusalem at every wedding, at every funeral, and at every bar mitzvah:

> If I forget you, O Jerusalem,
>> let my right hand forget its skill!
> Let my tongue stick to the roof of my mouth,
>> if I do not remember you,
> if I do not set Jerusalem above my highest joy! (Ps. 137:5–6 ESV)

This psalm was written from the vantage point of Babylon, but it is still remembered and chanted and treasured in Brooklyn. Again, this is the gravitational pull of Jerusalem—from the days of Esther until now.

But wait—this thing is even more complicated. The reason Zionists got initial support from Britain and continue to get a great deal of support from the United States, down to the present, is *also* a theological one, but coming from evangelical Christians who hold to a theology called *dispensationalism*. In this view, the reestablishment of Israel as a political entity (and the rebuilding of the temple) is a prophetic necessity in the unfolding of the end times. And so dispensational Christians have worked to help Israel in its formative years. When you combine the political influence of Jews in American politics, the influence of evangelical Christians in American politics, and the significant lack of anti-Semitism here, it is not surprising that Israel has a strong ally in the United States.

We have to sort this out in our minds and separate it from a theologically grounded Zionism. In an otherwise fine book on the threat posed by the rise of Muslim influence in Great Britain, journalist Melanie Philips said:

> The real motor behind the Church's engine of Israeli delegitimization is theology—or, to be more precise, the resurgence of a particular theology that had long been officially consigned to ignominy. This is "replacement theology," sometimes known also as "supercessionism," a doctrine going back to the early Church Fathers and stating that all God's promises to the Jews—including the land of Israel—were forfeit because the Jews had denied the divinity of Christ.[17]

The problem here is that historic Reformed and Lutheran theology holds that the church is the rightful heir of all the promises given to Israel, and dispensational Christianity does not. But it does not follow from this that we are anti-Semitic or that a disagreement with Christian Zionism requires us to want to uproot Israel *now*. A man can believe that the Nez Perce were badly treated without wanting to march all the current citizens of Idaho back to the East Coast. Whatever solution God wants us to find for this intractable problem, it will come to us where we are, not where we should have been.

When we are faced with a problem as difficult as this one, we look to continued support for Israel from the United States, aid to the Palestinians from Europe, or another stern resolution from the United Nations. But why do we look to these entities to solve the problem when they were the ones who *created* it in the first place? Britain governed Palestine under a mandate from an international body, the League of Nations. The United Nations sealed it in concrete (1948), and the United States has helpfully stepped in to take the grizzly bear by the ears, a position we occupy today. This looks like a political problem, but one without a political solution. The only real solution would appear to be spiritual.

> With the emergence of Zionism in the early twentieth century, the Muslims faced a "Jewish problem" for the first time since Mohammad. This time they faced it from a position of weakness, with the Jews for the first time since the destruction of the Temple poised to reestablish a polity that would be territorial as well as spiritual and cultural. The result was a massive outpouring of raw hatred, as atavistic and vitriolic as anything seen in Hitler's Germany, with the important difference that Nazism could not claim any scriptural grounding or divine mandate, even if it had wished for one.[18]

But hatred only breeds hatred, and bloodshed only sets the stage for the next round of bloodshed. Something drastic has to happen in the Middle East, something to make us rethink the value of violence in settling intractable disputes.

## THE LEGACY OF JERUSALEM

Having looked at the raggedy history of Jerusalem over the course of thousands of years, you may be tempted to check the cover of this book: *Five Cities That Ruled the World*. It looks as though this city has pretty much been ruled *by* the world. The last time Jerusalem was the capital city of a nation that was the envy of the other surrounding nations was about three thousand years ago. Since that time it has, in varying degrees, been the rope in a geopolitical tug-of-war, with different teams swapping in and out at each end of the rope. *Ruled* the world?

The legacy of Jerusalem is a spiritual one. The city has entered the spiritual consciousness of all history and all nations, and it has done so for all time. Of course, the *territory* of Jerusalem will remain a holy site for Muslims, and it will remain a holy city for devout Jews. With the exception of the Sea of Galilee, Christian pilgrims will continue to go to Jerusalem in order to walk where Jesus walked. All this is as it should be. Muslims, Jews, and Christians should be able to walk peacefully together in the streets of Jerusalem. And people will continue to live there, and there will be political upheavals in the future, just as there have been in the past. But none of this is the reason for the potency of Jerusalem's legacy.

Every time someone tells a pearly gates joke, he is referring—however obliquely—to the New Jerusalem. The same goes for all references to the golden streets. The story of Jerusalem's history, much of which we have considered here, is a central part of the biblical story, which means that Christian children—to the end of the world—will be reading about Abraham, David, Solomon, and Ezra. They will also read the account of how Jesus wept over Jerusalem and how He was crucified there. He also rose from the dead in that same place; because of this the new humanity will always consider Jerusalem its garden of Eden. The first garden is where it all started, but Jerusalem is where it all started *again*.

Because of this, the topography of Palestine, with Jerusalem in the center, has become the topography of our souls. When we come to the day of our death and we think about crossing Jordan, that metaphor indicates we are going west to Jerusalem. I remember being taught as a child that we should be like the Sea of Galilee and not like the Dead Sea. Both are fed by the same Jordan River, and yet, because the Dead Sea has no outlet, it is not conducive to life. The Sea of Galilee, on the other hand, is teeming with life. So, the lesson went that when you hear the Bible taught, it is like the Jordan coming into your sea. But you have to apply it, put it into practice. You have to have an outlet for what you learn—otherwise you are going to become a pretty salty character and things will float in your life that ought to sink. But we can certainly press the metaphor too far.

Abraham is the father of all who believe because of what he did on Mount Moriah when he took the knife in his hand to show how firmly he believed the promise of God. And since that time, every son of Abraham has come to faith with a knife in his right hand.

David sat in the house of God at Jerusalem, astounded at the promise that had been given to him. God had told him that his descendants would sit on the throne of David forever and ever. And in fulfillment, in Jesus, who was a son of David, David's throne has been transferred to the New Jerusalem in the heavenly places, and Jesus will reign there forever. Too many people think that *Christ* is Jesus' last name. But Christ is a title, meaning "Messiah" or "the Anointed One." If Jesus had a surname according to our custom, it would be Davidson. Jesus ben David, Jesus the son of David, Jesus Davidson. And this promise that there Jerusalem and finds its fulfillment in the New Jerusalem.

The Scriptures teach that believers in exile long for the restoration of Jerusalem. And the New Testament shows that believers can consider themselves to be in exile, even though they may live in physical Jerusalem. N. T. Wright commented on the potency of that metaphor in Jesus' time: "In Jesus' day many, if not most, Jews regarded the exile as still continuing."[18] Applying that as a continuing metaphor for the ailments of the church, we can echo Martin Luther and speak of the Babylonian captivity of the church. And individuals can follow the analogy. Everyone in bondage to sin is in a form of exile. And what is repentance from drunkenness, lust, covetousness, anger, or hatred but a decision to go home to Jerusalem?

Athens was a powerhouse, and in keeping with the theme of our discussion, what happened there in ancient times continues to affect us in the present day. Some of the earliest experiments with democracy occurred there, and we are fond of the commonplace that Athens is the birthplace of democracy. But the fact that it is a commonplace does not keep it from being true. *Many* truisms are true. Even so, Athens was not the kind of democracy that most of us would recognize today. And yet *without* the development of that democracy, it is hard to imagine our later democratic institutions taking root.

So we are dealing with a truism that does not represent the complete truth. Athenian democracy *has* been a model for many political thinkers down through the ages, and many of the coins we still use in contemporary political discourse were first minted in Athens. But those modern political thinkers who appeal to Athens so easily have been able to make their assertions unimpeded by the messiness of the way things actually *were* in ancient Athens. Democracy in a book is far cleaner than democracy on the ground, and the contributions that Athens made to modern democracy, while enormous, have *sometimes* been overstated.

Few inhabitants of Athens were actual participants in their democratic processes, and they had institutions like ostracism, which allowed their democracy to play a little rough. For example, they felt perfectly free with their custom of sending a prominent person into exile from the city, an exile not to exceed a period of ten years.[1] When we think of such a brutal custom, and we look at the range of prominent persons in our day who could perhaps benefit from this process, it fills us with a strange combination of civilized disapproval and pagan wistfulness.

Human sacrifice was relatively rare among the Greeks, but it was not unknown. Agamemnon sacrificed his daughter for the sake of favorable winds in order to sail against Troy. In fact, a whole class of individuals called *pharmakoi* provided a stable of available sacrifices as the need arose.[2] And so all this means that when we attribute words such as *democracy* and *freedom* to ancient Athens, we need to be careful to do so without importing our anachronistic understandings of these words.

At the same time, they used such words and had coherent concepts for them, which can surprise us as well. We have to be careful to avoid two extremes. One is assuming that the ancient Athenians were identical to us in every way, and the other is the mistake of assuming them to be completely alien. We can measure which error we are nearest by gauging our reaction to the information that the Athenians had several different words for "free speech." Not only that, but they felt free to name their ships *Democracy* and *Free Speech*.[3]

In recent years, it has become common for biblical theologians and writers to contrast the Hebraic way of thinking with the Hellenistic or Greek way of thinking, usually to the disadvantage of the Greeks. It is a reasonable point, as far as it goes, but at the same time it is easy to make too much of it. We need to remember that while there were significant Hebraic contributions, we must not minimize the role that Athens really did play. It is indisputable that we get a great deal of our civic tradition and terminology from the Greeks, and this is closely related to the contribution of reason that comes to us from Athens. It is no accident that the rise of democracy and the rise of philosophy occurred in the same era.

## THE FOUNDING OF ATHENS

"Greek myth and Greek art are inseparable," said historian Robert Bowie Johnson. "Greek art depicts the myth: Greek myth explains the art."[4] And Greek history is woven into the mix. Once we have our mix of myth and art and history, we then have the daunting task of interpretation.

The Greeks show up in the Bible fairly early. Noah had three sons—Ham, Shem, and Japheth (Gen. 10). Biblical scholars generally acknowledge that the sons of Japheth moved west and north, into Europe for the most part, and one ancestor of the Greeks is reputed to have been Iapheti. A possible connection to the biblical Japheth seems reasonable, particularly when we consider the names of Japheth's sons, one of whom was Javan. A common identification is that of Javan with the Ionians, one of the early Greek tribes. The word *Javan* is used in the Old Testament and is frequently rendered simply as *Greece*.[5]

We know very little about how the Ionians actually settled in what is now Greece. They were located in hundreds of small, independent city-states, and it was not until the Persian attempt to conquer them in the fifth century BC that anything like a pan-Hellenic identity started to develop.

The first to speak Greek in this area were the Mycenaeans. They should be thought of not as a separate ethnic group, but as the inhabitants of a markedly distinct period of early Greek history and culture. The Mycenaeans were to the later Greeks what the Elizabethans are to us. Agamemnon was the king of Mycenae, and the period of the great Homeric heroes was the Mycenaean era.

During the Mycenaean heyday—the fourteenth and thirteenth centuries BC—striking wealth was much in evidence. Kings were buried in fine tombs, and their palatial estates were magnificent. The pride of their culture was evident in the remains we have found of their stonework, not to mention the gold and silver treasures that have been uncovered. Theirs was a highly developed and hierarchical culture, one not shy about displaying its wealth.[6] At the same time, the government of these people was decentralized, just as it was centuries later. Despite Agamemnon's command of the forces against Troy, there was no one Mycenaean city that governed the others, not even Mycenae.

According to early stories, what later became the city of Athens had been originally a cluster of villages, brought together by Theseus. When dealing with some of these shadowy figures on the threshold of prehistory and history, my assumption is that they were usually men who really lived, but around whom many legendary stories later developed. Ambrose Bierce in *The Devil's Dictionary* cleverly defined *mythology* as "the body of a primitive people's beliefs concerning its origin, early history, heroes, deities and so forth, as distinguished from the true accounts which it invents later."[7] The most famous of the stories about Theseus is his voyage to Crete in order to kill the Minotaur in the labyrinth. The Minotaur seems clearly legendary, yet archeologists have found the ruins of the labyrinth. According to some later legends, Theseus also ended the control over the seas that King Minos of Crete had exercised previously.

The city of Athens was named after the goddess Athena, or perhaps the goddess took her name from the city. Athena, according to mythology, came out of the head of Zeus when Hephaestus attacked Zeus with an axe and split his head open. Athena sprang out ready for battle, which probably scared Hephaestus, at least a little bit.[8]

The great temple of Athena at the center of Athens was not built until centuries later (447 BC), after the victory over the Persians, but she had been the goddess of the city long before that time. Athena's most renowned place of worship, her temple on the Acropolis, was constructed on the site of the Mycenaean palace of Erechtheus, a character in *The Odyssey*.[9] The raising of that remarkable temple was the result of Pericles wanting to transform the purpose of the Delian League, but we'll get to that shortly.

## WAR WITH TROY

The fall of Troy is one of the most well-known stories of the ancient world. And while Troy is not Athens, it is this story that really introduces the Greeks to the world and sets the stage for most of our subsequent perceptions of them. The stories of

Homer were the stories of what amounted to the Athenians' "Bible." Most moderns know about Helen and about the Trojan Horse and who wound up winning that war. And most of us are familiar with Christopher Marlowe's line that Helen's was the "face that launched a thousand ships." Perhaps this might provide a modern scientific scale for measuring feminine attractiveness or beauty—.001 *helen* being a sufficient magnitude of beauty to launch one ship.

Priam was the king of Troy and his son Paris was a lover, not a fighter. But despite his lack of military prowess, he still managed to run off with the wife of the Greek Menelaus, a beautiful woman named Helen. This had come about because he had been pressed into duty as a judge in a beauty contest between three goddesses: Hera, Athena, and Aphrodite. Paris was in no position to decide between these goddesses, and so they all began offering him incentives.

Hera promised him power and authority over all Asia if she won. Athena (the goddess of Athens, remember) promised him great wisdom and prowess in battle if she won. But Aphrodite knew her business and her man, and promised him the most beautiful woman in the world if she won. Paris decided in her favor. The promised woman turned out to be Helen, and so Paris made off with her, perhaps with her consent and perhaps not. The stories range from consensual adultery to kidnapping and rape. The Trojans refused to return Helen to the Greeks, and ten years of fierce fighting followed.

So there was a common cultural identity among the Greeks as early as the Trojan War, but it was merely in a temporary military alliance that a number of the participants didn't want to be in. The summons to fight against Troy was extended not to the citizens of some entity called "Greece," but to individuals who had previously been suitors for the hand of Helen and who had sworn a personal oath to defend her honor—as a means of keeping the peace after she made her choice.

It is ironic that most of us know about the fall of Troy from Homer's epic *The Iliad* when that poem does not actually record the fall of Troy. The name of the poem comes from another name for Troy, which was Ilion. The epic is actually about the fall of the Greek hero Achilles into dishonor through his treatment of the body of the Trojan hero Hector. It is also (perhaps) about Achilles' recovery from that dishonor. At any rate, when the poem ends, the city of Troy is still standing.

In hearing this story, we recognize the larger questions of trade and economics and hegemonic honor in the background. Was a struggle of this magnitude really over Helen? Or was Helen the excuse? More than one war has erupted that way, where the stated cause of war was unrelated to the real causes. This war ended with the destruction of Troy as a political and economic force in the eastern end of the Mediterranean, and it seems at least plausible that this was the intended point all along. In Homer's story the destruction of Troy is a given.

Homer's other epic *The Odyssey* is about Greek civilization coming of age in the aftermath of the Trojan War. But there was a problematic time lapse. After the collapse of the Mycenaean culture, there were about three hundred years of the Greek Dark Ages. Homer wrote at the tail end of that period—let us say around 800 BC—when things were just starting to look up again, at the beginning of the Archaic period of Greek history.

Homer's story of Odysseus returning home was set as the Greeks were poised to fill the vacuum left by Troy. The Greeks had not filled this role earlier, but perhaps Homer was looking forward to the next great opportunity and telling the story as inspiration for his countrymen.

The story of this homecoming is a simple and satisfying adventure story, with Odysseus desperately seeking to get home again after the war and taking ten years to do it. But another issue is brooding in the background. In the run-up to the war with Troy, the Greeks were basically freebooting pirates. Smash-and-grab runs were the order of the day, and Troy was one of the largest prizes. The wealth of Mycenaean culture still depended on raids and warfare.

On his way back home, Odysseus was taken captive on the island of the goddess Calypso, and he was offered immortality and sexual bliss with her forever. Given how pirates are supposed to think, it is striking that he rejected all this in favor of an ordinary mortal life and a return to his people at home. This abandonment of what was essentially a short-term Viking-like lifestyle was the basis for the rise of long-term Greek civilization.

The war with Troy occurred around 1200 BC, which would mean Greek heroes—Odysseus, Agamemnon, Achilles, and the others—were contemporary with biblical heroes like Gideon, Samson, and Jephthah. It was the period after the Israelites' exodus from Egypt under Moses but before the monarchy was established under Saul and David. The account of these Greek heroes was provided by Homer, who lived around the eighth century BC, which made him a contemporary of the prophet Isaiah.

The Trojan War was consigned to the mists of antiquity and legend until the middle of the nineteenth century. In 1863, a British expatriate, Frank Calvert, was convinced that he had found the ruins of Troy in western Turkey. Five years later, a more famous individual named Heinrich Schliemann provided money for more digging, and he is usually credited with the discovery. The excavation of Troy reminds us how foolish it is to assume ancient history is nothing but myths and fables and that only modern historiographers can get it right.

## MARATHON AND SALAMIS

A handful of battles still astonish us with their momentous issues, overwhelming odds, and breathtaking courage. Examples include the English victory at Agincourt, the American triumph at Saratoga, and the Greek victory at Marathon. Marathon was a small battle, as battles go, but it was one of the most significant battles in the history of the world.

The famous story of Philippides running from the battlefield to Athens (a distance of just over twenty-six miles) to announce the victory is likely a conflation of several stories.[10] But on the basis of that story, a long-distance run from Marathon to Athens was included in the first round of the reestablished Olympic Games of 1896. A local Greek shepherd won that marathon, becoming a national hero as a result, and the concrete was set. Since then we have been running marathons like crazy. When we consider the story of the battle itself, these ongoing commemorations will make a bit more sense.

At Marathon in 490 BC, the cities of Athens and Plataea

stopped a Persian incursion instigated by Darius. Several points need to be made about what happened there. First, the victors were greatly outnumbered not only on the field of battle but also in a geopolitical sense. About ten thousand Greeks faced thirty thousand Persians,[11] and the Persian Empire extended from India in the east, across what is now Afghanistan, throughout Mesopotamia (which would include modern Iraq), across Egypt and Cyrene. Athens was just one small city, a little bit past the western Persian frontier. Second, the stakes were enormous and known to be enormous by those fighting. Today we can see that the stakes were even more momentous than the contending armies thought. Third, the outnumbered victors won not by blind folly or luck but by discipline and audacious courage. And fourth, when the armies collided, it was *personal*.

A strange series of events brought about the battle. The Athenian democracy was very young—the Athenians had expelled the tyrant Hippias in 510 BC. Hippias then went to the Persians and wanted them to reinstate him in his rule over Athens. Darius was emperor over all Persia, and his satrap (provincial governor) at Sardis was named Artaphernes. When the Athenians heard that refugees had gone to Sardis and were slandering those who had expelled the tyrant, they sent emissaries to counteract the stories. That didn't work. Artaphernes stated that if they were mindful of their own safety, they would receive Hippias again as their ruler. The Athenians indignantly rejected this declaration, and they believed a state of war existed between them and the Persians.

Some Ionian Greeks under Persian domination appealed to

the Greeks generally for help. Two cities—Athens and Eretria—responded; they sailed against Sardis and burned it. The raiders were pursued and destroyed by Persians, but the insult was not forgotten. The Greek historian Herodotus put it this way:

> News reached King Darius of the Athenian and Ionian capture and burning of Sardis. . . . It is said, however, that his first reaction to the news was to discount the Ionians, because he was confident of punishing them for their rebellion, and to ask who the Athenians were. On hearing the answer, he is said to have asked for his bow; he took hold of it, notched an arrow, and shot it up towards the sky. And as he fired it into the air, he said, "Lord Zeus, make it possible for me to punish the Athenians." Then he ordered one of his attendants to repeat to him three times, every time a meal was being served, "Master, remember the Athenians."[12]

Even more personal: when the Persian invaders arrived at Marathon, they brought along Hippias. Darius had required all Greek cities to send tokens of their submission as vassals to him. Most complied, but Athens and Sparta were feeling their mettle and refused.

The plain of Marathon is about six miles long, in a crescent shape. At its center the plain is about two miles across. The mountains come down close to the water at the horns of the crescent, and in the autumn—when this battle occurred—the tips of the crescent were marsh. The Persian navy had beached their ships as was customary, and they used islands behind them to store their supplies. The Athenians were up in the hills above the plain, trying to figure out what to do.

Ten generals were there, representing the various tribes of Athens. Callimachus was the elected war leader that year, and he broke a tie vote between the generals about whether to go down on the plain and confront the Persians. He voted in favor of the fight.

The hero of Marathon was Miltiades, one of the generals who urged immediate action against the Persians. He knew that if they sat there waiting for the Persians to make their move, opportunists on the Greek side would interfere. More than a few Greeks thought that resistance to the Persian forces was sheer, unadulterated madness.

Two of the other generals making the decision were Themistocles (future hero of the battle of Salamis) and Aristides, who would lead the Athenians at the battle of Plataea (which finally drove out the Persians). When Callimachus made the decision in favor of the counsel of Miltiades, it was decided that Miltiades would command the battle.

The Athenians descended, and the initial response from the Persians was one of amusement. According to Herodotus, when the Persians saw the Athenians—no cavalry, no archers, and pretty thin numbers—they thought they were encountering madmen intent on collective suicide. But the Athenians were disciplined fighters, and they were in shape. They ran in rank, contrary to the usual practice, for the mile or so that separated the foot of the mountains and the first Persian outposts.

Generally, the Athenians were accustomed to fight in a tight "platoon" about eight spears deep. But Miltiades made adjustments to this. Callimachus had command of the right flank. Themistocles and Aristides had command of the center, where Miltiades deliberately made their ranks thinner, beefing up the right and left flank instead.

When the armies closed, there was vigorous fighting, but the deliberately thin center of the Athenians was forced to give way. When the Persians drove toward the middle, the deeper Athenian flanks from both sides folded in upon them like a vise.

Many Greek fatalities, including Callimachus, occurred in the fighting at the water's edge, when the Greeks were trying to set fire to the Persian ships. They succeeded with only seven of them. The disparity was astonishing in the final tally of the dead, however. According to historian Edward Creasy, "The number of the Persian dead was 6,400; of the Athenians, 192."[13]

Datis, the commander of the Persian forces, sailed away, planning to head straight to Athens to take the city. But Miltiades, anticipating that move, led his victorious troops in a march by night to Athens.[14] Imagine Datis's surprise when the Persian fleet came into sight of Athens. He saw the men who had defeated him the day before lined up and prepared to defend their city. It was too much for him; the Persians returned to Asia.

The dead were buried on the field of Marathon. Their names were inscribed on a monument that a man named Pausanias was still able to read six hundred years later. The names are now long gone, but the mound remains. It is difficult to imagine how different human history would have been since that time if the Greeks had not prevailed. The Persian Empire was magnificent in scope and in wealth, but it was also despotic, with no tradition of liberty.

Looking back, we can see Marathon as the turning point, but obviously Darius did not view it that way. To him, the defeat of his troops was an embarrassing skirmish but not a decisive battle. He began planning immediately for a massive invasion. Preparations had to be broken off when Egypt rebelled against Persian authority in 487 BC. Two years later, Darius died, with Athens still beyond his reach. His son Xerxes took over and quelled the rebellion in Egypt. Then Persian attention turned once again to Athens.

When Xerxes ordered his invasion, ten years after Marathon, the Persians arrived in Greece en masse. The naval battle occurred at Salamis, mostly because the Athenians refused to fight any farther south and it was the only place where a pan-Hellenic navy could be held together long enough to maintain a fight. The odds against the Greeks were again overwhelming, and the resultant victory against the Persians was another remarkable event in military history. In a follow-up land battle the next year at Plataea (479 BC), the remaining Persian army was again defeated.

At Salamis, the Persian armada had more than 600 ships, and the Greeks probably had between 300 and 370 ships. Aeschylus, who fought both at Marathon and at Salamis, set the number of Persian ships much higher. He and Herodotus recorded that the Persian armada had more than 1,000 ships and 200,000 sailors. Historian Victor Davis Hanson pointed out that if this is accurate, the battle of Salamis involved the largest number of combatants "in the entire history of naval warfare."[15]

The difference between the forces (besides the size, which favored the Persians) was the command structure. The Persians had a tight top-down command and control system. The throne of Xerxes was established on the shore so that he could watch his victory from a position of high privilege, honor, and power. After the battle, some Persian admirals were upset with some Ionian Greeks who had deserted the Persian cause on the eve of battle, going over to their fellow Greeks. Xerxes was unhappy with their complaint and had the admirals decapitated.[16] When Pythius the Lydian took action on his own initiative, the king had his son cut in two.[17] Voltaire would later offer the advice that a king ought to hang an admiral from time to time in order to encourage the others. This *bon mot* was actually applied in deadly earnest by the Persians. The Greek system had its disadvantages, to be sure, sometimes verging on democratic anarchy, but in this situation it clearly worked.

Themistocles, the hero of the Greeks and a fighting admiral, sailed with his forces. The Greeks had a much more decentralized system of military governance than did the Persians, which meant that individual commanders had the authority to adapt to situations as they developed. Differences of opinion and counsel were aired freely.

Themistocles had sent false assurance to Xerxes that his forces would surrender on the eve of battle, which he then proceeded not to do. On his own initiative, Aristides landed on the island of Psyttaleia to attack the Persian garrison there. Greek triremes joined up with them at the last minute, including triremes that had deserted from the Persian side. According to Victor Davis Hanson, "All were individual and free acts done by those who themselves were used 'to do as they pleased.'"[18]

The lessons were not lost on a Greek historian like

Herodotus. Free men make much better fighters than conscripted slaves do. The Persian encroachment into Greek territory was stopped—and within a few generations, Alexander would reverse the entire balance of power, and the Persians would be unable to stop him.

## THE GOLDEN AGE

The aftermath of the defeat of the Persians at Salamis was a glorious time for Athens and ushered in its golden age (448 BC and years following). The historian Lewis Mumford stated that "participation in the arts was as much a part of the citizen's activities as service on the council or in the law courts, with their six thousand judges," and he described the twelve new tragedies performed annually, as well as sixteen new comedies. "In the hundred years of the Empire . . . two thousand plays of picked quality were written and staged in Athens, while six thousand new musical compositions were created and presented."[19]

Of course, pride goeth before the tumble down the geopolitical slope. But it was obvious to the Athenians at the time that they had something about which to be proud. Historian Donald Kagan noted the glory of this period in Athenian history:

It was a time of extraordinary cultural achievement, probably unmatched in its originality and fecundity in all of human history. Dramatic poets like Aeschylus, Sophocles, Euripides, and Aristophanes raised tragedy and comedy to a level never surpassed. Architects and sculptors created the buildings on the Acropolis in

Athens, at Olympia, and all over the Greek world that
influenced the course of Western art so powerfully and
still do so today. . . . It was a time of great progress, prosperity, and confidence. To all this the great conflict put
an end.[20]

The "great conflict" noted was the war between Athens and
Sparta, along with their respective allies—what we call the
Peloponnesian War. But before that war wreaked its havoc, the
vast concentration of cultural contributions in Athens could
hardly be overstated. The aesthetic and architectural influence
from this period continues to the present. Students in our uni-
versities still study the tragedies and comedies of the ancient playwrights. And philosopher Alfred North Whitehead said with
slight overstatement that the entire history of philosophy con-
sists of a series of footnotes to Plato.[21]

But the glory days of the arts came to an end because of
what was happening in the political realm. The Delian League
had originally been a bulwark against Persian aggression, but
Pericles had signed a treaty with the Persian enemy in 448 BC.
After this occurred, the Delian League quickly became an instru-
ment for Athens to dominate the other Hellenic cities. New circumstances can suggest the adaptation of an organization formed
by treaties for one purpose to another purpose entirely. This
adaptation can be creative adaptation or radical mission drift—
think NATO after the collapse of the Soviet Union. In this case,
the Delian League turned from the defense of all Greece, led by
Athens, to the glory and honor of Athens over the other Greek
cities, manipulated by Athens. As Athens acknowledged in its

plays from this period, hubris is the undoing of all. That the Athenians clearly knew this did not prevent it from happening to them.

Another important legacy is the structure of theater. Any serious study of the impact of Greek theater is incomplete if confined to the mere study or restaging of these ancient plays. Many basic theatrical devices that we use today grew directly out of the theater of that time.

The earlier heroes and kingdoms and adventures (1400–750 BC) provided the raw material for their themes and plots. That was the period in which the myths and stories developed that provided the pool from which later writers drew. And as is frequently the case when this kind of thing happens, the playwrights from Athens's golden era frequently told the old stories with a contemporary twist or point. (For a later example, there was trouble in Shakespeare's time with Queen Elizabeth's consternation over the staging of *Richard II*—a play in which a monarch is toppled is *calculated* to attract a monarch's attention.)

In these ancient Greek plays, fate outranked the gods and overruled them. This is a key point to understand—the gods, just like men, were subsets within the cosmos. The idea of the Creator/creature divide, which the Christian faith brought to us, would have been a strange idea to them. Fatalism was widespread. Divination was consequently significant—from inquiring of Apollo at Delphi to seeking portents from Zeus at Dodona. Within these plays the gods were frequently jealous of humans and made life difficult for them.

Put all of this together, and we have the cogs and wheels of the dramatic mechanism. Fate determined that Oedipus, for example, would kill his father and marry his mother. The play consisted of all the ways that Oedipus demonstrated the inevitability of his choices. His actions to avoid fulfilling his fate were the very actions that necessitated he would fulfill his fate.

The cult of Dionysus began to spread among the Greeks around 700 BC—and there was controversy about that growth. There is even a play about it. *The Bacchae* by Euripides describes the rise of devotion to Dionysus, the god of wine and drunken revelry, and the futility of resistance. But the influence of Dionysian worship did more than provide a subject for a play; it provided some of the structure for plays that we observe today. For example, the circular dancing place around the altar of Dionysus was called the *orchestra*. Dionysus was a suffering god, undergoing death and resurrection. Hence the worship alternated between the extremes of lament and ecstasy. A chorus of forty men in goat skins worshiped him, and as they did so, a story about Dionysus was improvised.

Thespis of Attica (ca. 550–500 BC) is called the father of the drama (hence our word *thespians* for actors). He created the first hypocrites, who performed between the dances of the chorus and who interacted with the leader of the chorus. The Greek word *hypocrite* referred to the masks worn by the actors and later assumed its modern meaning, for obvious reasons.

Stories about characters other than Dionysus were introduced eventually, and the chorus of goat-satyrs was replaced by a more general chorus. The *prologue* was the action before the chorus entered. The *episodes* were action between the choral odes.

The theater of Dionysus at Athens had a seating capacity of seventeen thousand. By necessity the builders must have possessed a solid knowledge of acoustics—there was obviously no amplification, the actors were talking through masks, and people in the back of the theater wanted to hear what was going on. And there was probably a guy two rows in front of them who was coughing like crazy, and they didn't have throat lozenges.

Friedrich Nietzsche wrote his first book—*The Birth of Tragedy*—discussing the tension created between the orderly, rational worship of Apollo and the frenzied, frantic worship of Dionysus. His thesis was that this glorious art form of tragedy was a synthesis born out of the tension between these two forms of worship and the culture based on that worship.[22] Cultures *do* tend to alternate between the Apollonian and the Dionysian. In our day, just think of the 1950s and '60s, when America had the laid-back Eisenhower attitude and how all that ended in 1968 when somebody let all the monkeys out of the cage. The Apollonian gave way to the Dionysian.

During the neoclassical period (roughly the seventeenth century and first part of the eighteenth), the Georgian architecture placed the highest premium on symmetry; Alexander Pope wrote compelling poetry, but he did it to a metronome; and Jane Austen got away with writing a lot more in the passive voice than aspiring writers in creative writing workshops nowadays are allowed to do. But this Apollonian period gave way to the Dionysian revolt of the Romantics, giving us poets Lord Byron and Percy Bysshe Shelley, and the musician Richard Wagner, and a host of lesser talents. In fact, the Dionysian revolt of the Romantics against the neoclassical forms had much to do with the rebirth of Athens in the nineteenth century, just as the development of the cult of Dionysus contributed to its initial establishment as a great city.

Ironically, Athenian comedies still work—and largely in the way they did then. But the Greek ideal for tragedy has been turned around by the growth of the Christian faith. T. S. Eliot observed that tragedy in the ancient sense is not really possible after the incarnation. We can have tragedies of a sort—there are lots of bodies at the end of *Hamlet*—but this is not the same as the fatalistic tragedies of the Athenian playwrights. As Macbeth disintegrates, we are observing the damnation of a soul. When Pentheus is torn apart by his mother and aunts in their bacchic frenzy, we are watching (among other things) how fate works its way to its inexorable end. The world of tragedy is very different. But when Aristophanes sends up Socrates in a farce called *The Clouds*, the story is still laugh-out-loud funny. After you read it, it is easy to believe that all philosophers ought to be exiled to a "thinketeria."

## AN UNKNOWN GOD

The great plague in the sixth century BC was devastating to Athens. It occurred just a short time before the great battles I have described. The plague was horrible, and the Athenians had done everything they could think of to stop it. They had propitiated every god—or so they thought. Still they experienced no relief. In their helplessness and confusion, they sent to the Pythian oracle at Delphi to inquire, "What god have we offended? How may we propitiate him?"

The oracle was famous for her cryptic answers, and this time was no exception. She said there was another god who remained unappeased, but she seemed unclear about the god's identity. She did say one clear thing—if they went to Knossos, located on the island of Crete, they would find a man there named Epimenides. If they brought him to Athens, he would know what to do and how to deliver the city from the plague.

The Pythian oracle took her name from the legend in which the god Apollo had come down and slain a giant python at Delphi. The priestess there—a pythoness—was dedicated to Apollo. So the Athenians did what the oracle had told them to do, and they sent for him. According to Plato, Epimenides was one of the great men who helped mankind recover various inventions lost during the Great Flood. The apostle Paul would later quote this same man in his epistle to Titus.

When Epimenides came to Athens, he had them take a flock of white and black sheep, and release them on Mars Hill early in the morning to graze. Epimenides instructed the Athenians to mark the place where any sheep lay down to rest, which would be unusual for hungry sheep so early in the morning. Epimenides wanted the god they were seeking to propitiate to indicate his willingness to receive certain animals as a sacrifice through this unusual means. Epimenides told the Athenians that they could offer sacrifices to this unknown god if they honestly confessed their ignorance and asked him for mercy.

And that was what they did. They confessed their ignorance and offered up these sheep on altars built for this purpose. The next morning the plague had abated, and within a week, the city had recovered. When the apostle Paul came to Athens centuries later, and found it teeming with idols, he found an altar from the time of Epimenides and told them he perceived "that in every way you are very religious. For as I passed along and observed the objects of your worship, I found also an altar with this inscription, 'To the unknown god.' What therefore you worship as unknown, this I proclaim to you."[23]

In this famous sermon on the Areopagus, the great apostle referred explicitly to men like Epimenides and those Athenians who had listened to him. They were "feel[ing] their way toward [God]." Paul told the crowd that God "is actually not far from each one of us" and argued the point using two familiar quotations: "'In him [God] we live and move and have our being'; as even some of your own poets have said, 'For we are indeed his offspring.'"[24]

The second quotation is from a poem by the pagan writer Aratus—"Phainomena." The first is probably from Epimenides himself. If so, Paul was quoting a previous deliverer of Athens to the Athenians, in the hope of seeing them delivered once again. This is important because when Paul came to Athens, he was preaching in a city with a long tradition of reliance on reason. Paul confronted the philosophers there, but he did not do so by insisting that the Athenians drop their entire heritage— he knew their history well enough to appeal to it in support of his case.

According to Plato, on this same visit to Athens that saw the cessation of the plague, Epimenides had prophesied that the Persian Empire would come against Athens in ten years and that the Persians would be turned back frustrated.

## SOCRATES, PLATO, AND ARISTOTLE

The Athenian intellectual influence has been profound. By raising and pressing certain questions, the philosophers managed to create an extremely dynamic—some might say unstable—intellectual tradition.[25] The result has nevertheless been an enormous source of intellectual creativity.

To make sense of the impact of Greek philosophy, we need to note a general assumption about the world that was common among the Greeks. (But we should not take this word "common" to mean universal.) We inherited it largely through the influence of Socrates, Plato, and Aristotle, all men from this same period.

The assumption is that the realm of matter is a lower-story realm, and the realm of the mind is an upper-story realm. The realm of matter was generally despised, and the life of the mind, exalted. The philosopher would not use his intelligence to make a pile of money or build a clever invention, but would devote himself to thinking great thoughts in the realm of pure abstraction. The philosophers wanted life in Euclidville, my nickname for the pristine realm of the mind, named after the Greek father of geometry. And even Euclidville had strict building codes—the lines had to have no width, the points no length, and the planes no height. It was life on the chalkboard, with no chalk dust.

One of the best examples was the attitude of Archimedes (287– ca. 212 BC) toward the war machines that he was asked to build. He much preferred the life of the mind. He did not want to bring himself down to the level of moving matter around. Nevertheless, in the defense of his native city, he did it very well. He engineered Archimedes' claw, a device that was capable of picking up approaching Roman ships and turning them over.

The Roman historian Livy recorded that Archimedes was killed during the sack of Syracuse by a Roman soldier who did not know who he was. There should have been clues—Archimedes was oblivious to the tumult in the city around him and was distracted by mathematical figures he had been drawing in the dust. Caught up in the excitement of his math problem (and what is the sack of your city compared to *that*?), he paid no attention to the soldier and was promptly slain.

According to the Athenian philosophers, the world of universals was the real world; this shadowy world full of particular things was less real. The philosophers did not concern themselves with these things. The material world got in the way of the philosophical endeavor, like wet clay on your thinking boots. Enlightened philosophers had learned to "step around" all the distractions.

Aristotle was a pupil of Plato, and Plato had been a student of Socrates. Socrates obviously had an enormous impact on them and the rest of us, but we know very little about his life. Part of the reason is that Socrates wrote nothing, and everything we have of his teaching is filtered through the writing of Plato.[26] Plato's dialogues record conversations between his master Socrates and other partners in conversation; and Socrates, by his patient and persistent questioning, usually rolled their socks down and pulled their togas over their heads. But since all this comes to us through Plato, we are not quite sure how much is the thought of Socrates and how much is the thought of Plato. Historian of philosophy Richard Tarnas offered a likely scenario:

> Beginning with the *Phaedo*, and in fully developed form in such dialogues as the *Symposium* and the *Republic*, the character of Socrates increasingly voices positions that move beyond those attributed to him in the earlier dialogues and by other sources such as Xenophon and Aristotle. Although the evidence may be interpreted in several ways, it would appear that Plato, in reflecting upon the legacy of his teacher in the course of his own intellectual evolution, gradually made explicit in these more developed positions what he understood to be implicit in both Socrates's life and his arguments.[27]

In the thought of Plato, the realm above was the realm of the Forms. All the chairs down here were what they were because they somehow partook of ultimate Chairness, the Form of Chair in the universal realm. And the same goes for the table and the forks and the spoons. This idea tended to perpetuate a fundamental division between the realms. A consistent problem for Platonists is how to tie the two realms together: How do all the chairs down here "plug into" the Chair?

For Aristotle, everything in the world was a combination of Form and matter, so for him, the Chairness of the thing was resident within all the chairs, making them what they were. In his painting *The School of Athens*, Raphael portrayed Socrates reclining on the stairs (perhaps), with Plato and Aristotle walking side by side. Plato is pointing upward to the heavens, and Aristotle is pointing down, a good parable for where each believed the Forms or essence of each particular thing resided.

For most of Western philosophical history, the thought of Plato was dominant until Aristotle made a comeback under the sponsorship of Thomas Aquinas in the medieval period. Interestingly, the writings of Aristotle had been preserved by the Muslims until Thomas Aquinas picked them up and put them back into circulation.

But for both Aristotle and Plato, the basic assumption was that the essence of a thing was what matters, and that the appearance of the thing in the world as we see it was nothing more than an accident, superfluous to the definition of the thing. Western culture has consequently been characterized by an assumption that everything that matters can be defined with precision and anything that cannot be so defined must not matter that much.[28]

Everything had to be defined—and defined without reference to its antecedents. The definition of *bird* had no relation to a particular bird. This has led to a certain detachment from the world of stuff, or disparagement of it. In the second century AD this general Hellenistic turn of mind became a problem in the early church because of the Gnostic challenge, which translated this bias against matter in the name of reason into spiritual terms. Gnostics believed the realm of the spirit was clean and pure, and the realm of matter was permanently contaminated.

The Christian church specifically rejected this Hellenizing tendency, most notably at the Councils of Nicea and Chalcedon. For the church to affirm as it did that the ultimate Truth and Reality became a living, breathing man—having ten toes, ten fingers, the works—was mortally offensive to the sophisticated Greek mind.

This is not to say that the Greek emphasis had no impact on the church at all. Vestiges of Platonic thought can be found in varying degrees in many theologians of the early church, including Justin Martyr, Origen, and even Augustine.[29] The era of the New Testament was affected by this Greek culture, even though the political rulers at the time were the Romans.

The relationship between the Romans and the Greeks was interesting. Although the political and imperial zenith of the Greeks had been centuries earlier, Greek *culture* still held pride of place. The Mediterranean world of that era is called the Greco-Roman world for this reason. The relationship between the Romans and the Greeks was comparable to that today between the Americans and the British. The Americans have a lot of money, political power, imperial influence, and practical know-how, and shoot space shuttles off the planet in every direction, but the Brits provide what is popularly considered to be the gold standard of culture and learning. In a similar way, the Romans tended to defer to Greek philosophy, art, and poetry. This is why the language of commerce throughout the Roman Empire was Greek. This is why the New Testament was written in Greek instead of Latin. It was a Hellenistic world ruled by Romans.[30]

Diogenes the Cynic was a contemporary of Plato, and his antics were so extreme that one could almost suspect that he had received a grant from the National Endowment for the Humanities. He famously walked around Athens in broad daylight with a lantern, looking for "an honest man." One time in

Corinth, Diogenes had an encounter with Alexander the Great, who was very pleased to meet the philosopher. Diogenes was relaxing in the morning sun, and when Alexander asked what he could do for him, Diogenes replied, "Stand out of my sunlight." In another story, Alexander found Diogenes rummaging through a pile of bones and asked what he was doing. Diogenes replied that he was looking for the bones of Alexander's father but could not tell them apart from those of a slave. He was taking this basic Greek impulse—contempt for the tangible world—and running it out to the end of the road.

He was willing to do the most outrageous things to make his points. He defecated and urinated in public—and worse—and he did it all deliberately to offend the customs of decency, which he regarded as necessarily hypocritical. In most stories, he is usually the one with the snappy comeback and is the master of the situation. But not always. One time Plato got the better of him in the comeback department: "Diogenes came to Plato's house one day and was disgusted to find rich and exquisite carpets on the floor. To show his contempt he stamped and wiped his feet upon them, saying, 'Thus do I trample upon the pride of Plato.' 'With greater pride,' observed Plato mildly."[31]

## THE LOST YEARS

As long as Rome stood, Athens had a place of cultural honor. The Romans looked up to and respected Greek learning, and they appropriated it for their own. But after the fall of Rome, Athens ceased to be a player in world events, and in the world of geopolitics it was passed from hand to hand.

At first Athens was a city in the eastern half of the Roman Empire—what we call the Byzantine Empire. Things were pretty spotty after that. The Athenians were governed by the Franks for a while, as well as by the Catalans—Spanish mercenaries—and certain Florentines. The whole sad business culminated in the rule of Athens by the Ottoman Turks.

Yet the influence of this city has been considerable quite apart from armies, popes, and parliaments. Many ideas that were birthed in Athens were loose in the world—and the impact of those ideas was part of the reason why others were ruling in Athens.

Sometimes during these lost years (from the third century AD to the nineteenth), Athens prospered after a fashion, but never as a great city. Most of the time, Athens was not much more than an impoverished little town, with a population in the handfuls of thousands surrounded by amazing ruins.

Things started to go badly when the Goths—beginning their predations of Rome—included Athens in the business. They sacked Athens in the third century AD, and although they were driven out afterward, we can easily mark the decline of the city from that point. But because the schools remained there, the city of Athens was a pagan holdout in the face of the increasing Christianization of the empire. Two of the greatest church fathers in the East—Basil of Caesarea and Gregory of Nazianzus—were educated there by pagan rhetoricians. The emperor who sought to take the Roman Empire back into paganism, Julian the Apostate, was also instructed there.[32]

The church in Athens started slowly. The first church sanctuary was not built there until the first part of the fifth century, when it was built by a native-born Athenian woman named Aelia Eudokia.[33] This was due to the influence of the pagan schools, the bread and butter of Athens's intellectual and theological life.[34] These schools were the last functioning vestige of Athens's classical past, and they managed to survive until AD 529. The famous Parthenon was converted into a church of the Virgin Mary. In the years to come, it would also contain a mosque and a munitions dump.

Modern readers may have a hard time understanding the fluidity of the political situation. There were no borders in the modern lines-on-a-map sense, and it was fairly common for outposts of one culture to thrive deep within the "borders" of another. At one point, the pagan Slavs arranged to have the Byzantine leaders distracted by the Persians, and they swept down on Athens and annihilated the city (AD 582). It would be several centuries before the city got back on its feet.[35]

In the eighth century AD, the city produced a remarkable woman named Eirene. She went to Constantinople in 769 to marry the heir of the throne, Leo IV, but he died within a few years. She was about twenty-five years old at the time of her husband's death, and she—in defiance of custom—proclaimed herself regent and co-emperor until her nine-year-old son was ready to take the throne.

It would be nice to hold this story up as an example of a young girl's pluck and resolve in the face of numerous adversities, but to do that we would have to ignore the fact that Eirene was a talented but terrible woman. In any reference to the intricacies of Byzantine politics, her name should come to mind. She was not about to depart from power peacefully, and her son had to foment unrest in the army to get himself declared sole emperor about ten years later. Then seven years after that, because her son had no male heir and had become unpopular with the people, she managed to have him deposed and blinded. A few years later, she was banished to the island of Lesbos, one more true *character* in the thick annals of power grasping.

By the thirteenth century, the Franks had become a force in the world, and some of them came to Greece. Because of their slaughter of the inhabitants of Constantinople in 1204, they were not exactly received as liberators. They were quintessentially *Western*, and they did not fit into the Greek landscape at all. These armored knights loved jousting, falconry, and the whole bit. They ruled as the dukes of Athens for about a century.

A band of marauding mercenaries from Spain then entered the picture. The Catalans had been hired because Constantinople wanted them to fight the Turks, which they did for a while. When the leader of this mercenary force—"the renegade Templar Roger de Flor"[36]—was assassinated, the Catalans went on a tear of reprisals against their recent employer. They teamed up with the Turks and defeated the Franks in a pitched battle in 1311. The Catalans lasted as the masters of Athens for less than a century because a new round of mercenaries came in from Florence and took Athens away from them in 1388.

The next major transfer occurred with the arrival of the Ottoman Turks. After they conquered Constantinople, the outlying edges of the Byzantine Empire soon became what was known as European Turkey. Athens was taken by the Muslims, and a mosque was established in the Parthenon. The Orthodox

Christians there suffered under Muslim rule, but the Muslims labored to keep tensions alive between the Christians in the West and the Christians in the East. That was not hard to do—the feelings still ran high over the crusaders' sack of Constantinople in 1204. And recent occupation by the Catholics didn't help either.

The Turks held sway from the fifteenth through the eighteenth centuries. The zenith of Turkish influence was in the middle of the seventeenth century; after that, things began to slide for them. During that time, the Venetians besieged Athens. The Turks occupied the Acropolis as their natural fortress, and the Venetians set up their artillery on an opposing hill. Having received word that the Turks were storing their gunpowder in the Parthenon, the attackers aimed for it and, penetrating the roof, blew the thing sky high.

In the nineteenth century, tourists from the West made their way to Athens. They were antiquarians and amateur archaeologists with their eyes on the main chance. One of the most infamous was Lord Elgin, who made off with big chunks of the Parthenon. These priceless artifacts, known as the Elgin marbles, are now in the British Museum and, naturally, the Greeks want them back, which is unlikely to happen. Once the former colonial powers start returning things, who knows where it will stop?

In an ironic twist, it was in part the taking of the Elgin marbles to England that resulted in the liberation of Greece from the Turks. The arrival of Greek antiquities in England, and the exhibition of them, caused a sensation. It became glaringly obvious that the artwork of the ancient Greeks was of a very high

order indeed, and the previous assumption that Roman handi-
work was superior fell by the wayside. A movement made up of
*philhellenes*, admirers of all things Greek, captured the imagination of the West and forced their governments into a grudging
support of Greek independence from Turkey.[37]

A leading figure in this *philhellene* movement was George
Noel Gordon—the poet Lord Byron. When he came of age, he
began leading a seriously dissipated life. This lifestyle had a
number of results, but one of them was to create a deep desire
to do *something* worthwhile. In 1810, he and a friend named
Hobhouse went to Greece (which enchanted Byron), and Byron
swam the Hellespont at the site of Troy in imitation of Leander.
"Byron and Hobhouse crossed the Gulf of Lepanto to land at
the foot of Parnassus and visit Delphi before proceeding to
Athens. . . . Greece induced in him a sense of homecoming that
was to haunt him his life long."[38]

Byron was a Romantic, one who sized up the moment cor-
rectly and helped to establish the ideal of ancient Athens as a
Romantic ideal—something quite different from what Athens
had been during its heyday. Like many dissolute men, Byron
had dreams of "martial splendor" that would justify having such
a loser life. Unlike many dissolute men, he actually made an
attempt at it. Through the family of one of his many mistresses,
Byron made contact with a revolutionary society called the
Carbonari. Byron was very aware that he was not doing much to
justify his continued existence, and so he wanted to do something really noble that would vindicate him back in England
(where his reputation was pretty much shot). But of course, the
definition of that word *noble* was directed by the revolution-

ary and Romantic sentiments that were in the air everywhere. The revolutionary sentimentalism of Romantic idealism was readily projected back onto the glory that was Greece.

When the London Greek Committee asked Byron to act as its agent in helping along the Greek war for independence against the Turks, Byron joined the cause with enthusiasm. He chartered a ship, put up his own money, and sailed for Greece.

He spent the rest of his life trying to get the Greeks organized. He devoted a lot of time to preparing for war, but he died before battle actually transpired. To the Greeks, he was a hero and his death became a rallying point for them. After Greece attained independence, Byron's efforts were credited as an important part of the effort.

In many ways, the Greece that lives on in the minds of moderns is this resurrected Greece, as it was resurrected in the idealism of men like Byron. There is a real sense of glory, but it is the comic-book glory of the recent movie *300*, telling the story of the three hundred Spartans who stood against the Persians at Thermopylae. The outlines of the story are there, but the context and connotations are almost entirely wrong. Nevertheless, the stories of ancient Greece *are* still being told, and the truer influence of the Greeks—in mathematics, philosophy, and architecture—continues unabated.

## THE LEGACY OF ATHENS

We can resolve this apparent tension, getting away from the Romantic ideal of Greece, if we take a more accurate image from the apostle Paul when he was considering the growth of the kingdom of God in the world. If the Hebraic trunk was an olive tree, God had determined to take a number of wild olive branches from the Gentile world and graft them in. This kind of grafting produces, necessarily, a new kind of olive. In Romans 11, the great apostle used this image to describe the influx of Gentiles into the Christian church. And right at the center of the Gentiles who were on Paul's mind were the Greeks:

> Testifying both to Jews *and to Greeks* of repentance toward God and of faith in our Lord Jesus Christ . . . I am under obligation both *to Greeks* and to barbarians, both *to the wise* and to the foolish . . . But to those who are called, both Jews *and Greeks*, Christ the power of God and the wisdom of God . . . Give no offense to Jews *or to Greeks* or to the church of God . . . For in one Spirit we were all baptized into one body—Jews *or Greeks*, slaves or free—and all were made to drink of one Spirit.[39]

So the New Testament says quite a bit about the Greeks. Paul clearly had Greeks on his mind and used the illustration of a Hebrew trunk with many Greek branches. Even though Roman arms had triumphed in the Mediterranean world, Greek culture was still very much at the cultural center, and anyone who wanted to attain to the status of the educated elite had to deal with the Greeks. And at the very center of Greek culture and life was the city of Athens.

The early church father Tertullian complained that Jerusalem and Athens should have nothing in common. But this was too austere—it appears that according to the apostle Paul, a certain amount of cross-pollination was going to occur. The intellectual discipline that characterized Athens can be a good thing if it is not left to govern itself autonomously. Reason is a noble pursuit. And it remains a fact that this legacy inherited from Athens was a legacy that has been for the most part kept alive in the Christian West.

Of course, we want to approach this with wisdom because there can be no syncretistic accommodation between the God of Abraham and the gods that, as that same apostle would put it, "are not gods." God did not want His children worshiping Zeus and Hera. But He *did* determine that the New Testament, recording the culmination of all the messianic promises, should be written in Greek. And God did what He did because He *wanted* the olives to taste different. This is just another way of saying that Christians were called to acquire a taste for Greek food.

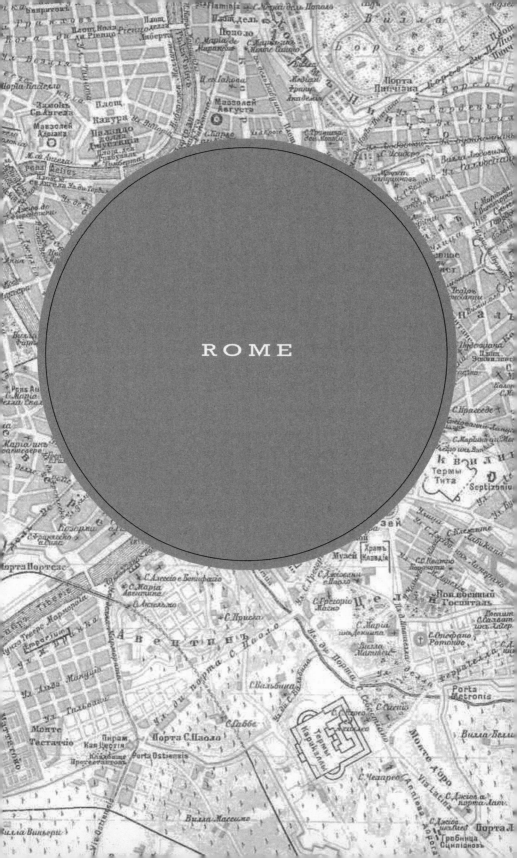

ROME

## FOUNDED IN BLOOD

Rome was fortunate enough to have had *two* famous foundings. One is the story as told by Virgil, as he was commemorating the refounding of Rome in the empire under Augustus. He told the story of Aeneas's flight from Troy and how his divine destiny had led him to Italy, which would have happened in the immediate aftermath of the Trojan War, which is commonly placed at 1184 BC. Another famous legend is about the twins—Romulus and Remus—and how Romulus built the walls of the city of Rome in the middle of the eighth century BC.

Telling Virgil's story first would seem most appropriate. Aeneas was a Trojan warrior who escaped from the destruction of Troy with his son and father, along with a small entourage. His wife was lost in the flight from the city, and although Aeneas attempted to go back and find her, he was unsuccessful. He was then led out of the city by a vision that promised him a brilliant future.

The epic poem by Virgil was intended to glorify the fulfillment of that prophecy in the rise to power of Caesar Augustus, who found the city of Rome built of brick, as he put it, and left it in marble. Virgil was writing at the dawn of this great empire, and he needed a splendid founding that was worthy of such a rebirth. The Roman Republic had lost its moorings, and some citizens saw the transition to empire as a glorious and necessary move. As such a move, it needed a mythology to match.

Aeneas launched his wanderings in order to find the spot that was his appointed destination. In his travels, he came to the site of Carthage, then under construction and ruled by Queen Dido. Dido was a Phoenician princess from the city of Tyre. To put this in context, just think of her as *some* kind of relative to another Phoenician princess from Tyre who settled somewhere else, farther to the east—a woman named Jezebel.

Aeneas had an affair with Dido and would have been happy to settle in Carthage but was forced by the divine will to leave. Dido was furious, cursed Aeneas, and then committed suicide, thus beginning the long-standing enmity between Rome and Carthage.

At last Aeneas reached Italy, and the gods arranged for him to marry Lavinia, the daughter of a local king named Latinus. All Latin students everywhere should know more about their namesake. Another suitor for the hand of Lavinia, a hero named Turnus, stirred up the local population, and there was a short war between the native Etruscans and the newly arrived Trojans. When the war was settled in favor of the Trojans, one term of the peace was that the Trojans would abandon the name of Troy in order to mollify the wrath of Juno (or Hera, as the Greeks called her). Juno had been told that the Romans would eventually defeat her beloved Carthaginians, and she had been trying to thwart that all along. At the end, she begrudgingly agreed for Troy to rise again, but she insisted that it *not* be under the former hated name.

The Trojans and the locals came together as one people, and things were relatively calm for centuries. But by the eighth century BC, two brothers—Numitor and Amulius, who were descendants of Aeneas—were contending for the throne. Numitor was the rightful king, but Amulius had control of the treasury and was able to usurp his brother's position. Numitor's daughter was named Rhea Silvia. Because Amulius was afraid that she would produce a male heir who could threaten his position, he forced her to become a vestal virgin. She was found to be with child anyway—the legends say that the father was Mars—and so she was executed and her twin boys were to be exposed to the elements. Instead of this, a servant—one scarcely knows why servants are always entrusted with these things, because they never do what they are told—built a small cradle for the twins and placed them in the Tiber River. They floated downstream until the cradle stopped in the roots of a fig tree. The river god Tiber then took them up to the top of the Palatine Hill, where they were famously suckled by a wolf and afterward found by the shepherd Faustulus, who brought them up as his own sons.

As the boys grew, their nobility became increasingly evident. They were finally restored to their grandfather Numitor and helped depose and kill their granduncle Amulius. They refused to rule as kings in Alba Longa as long as Numitor was alive, but they also refused to live there as his subjects. They settled on the Palatine Hill (one of the famous seven hills of

Rome) and established a colony there for various thugs, grifters, wastrels, runaway slaves, and scoundrels. (The founding of Rome had more than a little bit in common with the settling of the state of Georgia and the country of Australia.)

When they prepared to build the wall of Rome, a dispute arose about the best location. Romulus wanted it on the Palatine, while Remus contended for another hill. They decided to settle the dispute by augury—bird watching with a point—and Romulus saw more eagles (or vultures) than did Remus. But Remus saw his *first*, and the dispute continued. Romulus began work on the wall where he wanted it, and Remus mocked the efforts, tried to obstruct some of the work, and finally jumped across the trench that had been made for the wall. That was an omen of really bad luck, meaning the wall could easily be breached, and Remus was killed as a result.

The accounts vary about the killer, whether it was Romulus, a man named Fabius, or a fellow named Celer. One ambiguous account indicates that a group may have done the deed. The rivalry between the brothers (like the rivalry between their grandfather and his brother) ended in bloodshed, and Rome had what so many great empires have had—a founding murder. As Rene Girard has shown repeatedly in his studies of ancient civilizations, founding murders are common in the history of virtually all societies, and so are the corresponding founding mythologies, intended to serve as discreet veils over the bloodshed. It would be hard to inspire schoolchildren through the ages if John Adams had killed George Washington in order to take his place. And if he *had* done that, you can be sure that there would be an edifying story about how it all happened in a way that would keep the civilization, founded on blood, perceived as a noble endeavor.

## KINGS AND REPUBLIC

Ancient Rome had two periods of glory. One consisted of its rise to greatness in the period of the republic (ca. 509 BC and lasting about 450 years), and the other was the splendor and decadence of the empire (42 BC to AD 476). The Romans' ancient history, before the republic, was the time of rule by kings. When they finally threw off the tyranny of the kings, they developed such a deep antipathy to the very idea of monarchy that even Julius Caesar had to watch what he called himself. His absolute rule was okay in substance, but if he took on himself the prerogatives of royalty, then he was going to be in trouble. This antimonarchical bent of the Romans was very similar to the prejudices of modern Americans. We would all go sideways if one of our presidents had himself crowned, but modern American presidents have vastly more power over their "subjects" than King George III ever dreamed of having.

The Roman kings had gotten a bad name from the misbehavior of their seventh and last king, Lucius Tarquinius Superbus, or Tarquin the Proud (ruled 534–509 BC). He and his wife had engineered the overthrow and subsequent assassination of the previous king. There had been some developing constitutional reforms anticipating the coming republic, and Tarquin was a reactionary wanting to rule as an absolute despot. He did that until the Roman people exiled him and washed their hands of kings forever—or so they thought.

One of Tarquin's lasting legacies was his acquisition of the Sibylline Oracles—and at a pretty steep price. A woman, who turned out to be the Sibyl from Cumae near Naples, showed up incognito one day and offered to sell Tarquin nine books of prophecies for a tidy sum. He refused. She burned three of the books and made the offer again for the same price as before. He declined again, and she repeated her performance. This left her with three books, which she again offered for the same price as the original nine. Tarquin gave in and bought the books. He placed them in the temple of Jupiter on the Capitoline Hill, to be consulted only in emergencies, in order to keep Rome strong.

The books *were* consulted and obeyed from time to time. After the disastrous battle of Cannae in the Second Punic War (which we will discuss shortly), it was determined that the oracles required human sacrifice of two Gauls and two Greeks; the four individuals were buried alive in the marketplace. Caesar Augustus had the books moved to the temple of Apollo, and they were not destroyed until AD 405 by a Christian general.

During the last century of the republic, the century just before the Christian era, Rome was racked by civil war.[1] The transitions from the kings to the republic, and then from the republic to the empire, seemed necessary at the time. When the kings became oppressive, a republic looked really good. But when things started to go badly in the republic, it was easy to long for decisive, one-man rule. Interestingly, the republic got into trouble not because of Roman decadence but because of various catastrophes that came upon the people.[2] In some ways, the Romans' *virtues* got them in trouble.

## FIGHTING WITH THE PUNICI

The Punic Wars (called so because of the ancestors of the Carthaginians, the Punici) established the Roman Republic as a formidable power. Rome's primary rival was the Phoenician city of Carthage on the north coast of Africa, the city of the bereft Dido. The First Punic War (264–241 BC) resulted in the defeat of Carthage, but not its destruction. The Second War (218–201 BC) was made memorable by the exploits of Hannibal, who exhibited the same kind of military genius in Italy that Stonewall Jackson displayed in the Shenandoah Valley. But the more Hannibal fought in Italy, the more resolute Roman resistance became. Scipio prevailed against the city of Carthage, and this forced the withdrawal of Hannibal from the Italian peninsula—he had never lost a battle, but his people still lost the war. The Third Punic War (149–146 BC) ended with the utter destruction of Carthage.

Hannibal, whose full name (Hannibal Barca) meant "Grace of Baal Lightning," had held a deep enmity toward Rome since he was a small boy.[3] In the Second Punic War, he led his troops in annihilating the Roman forces during the battle of Cannae. Hannibal managed to ambush the Romans by tactical means on a plain in broad daylight. He arranged his troops in a crescent, with the convex of the arc facing the Romans. The Romans came against them, and inexplicably the Roman column was about thirty to fifty men deep, which meant only the first rows of men could actually fight. The intent was apparently to break through the Carthaginian ranks like a pile driver and then do the fighting afterward.

Hannibal's strategy was similar to what the Greeks had done at Marathon. He put his weakest troops in the center and stayed there with them to keep them from breaking. When they began falling backward before the Romans, the flanks of "Hannibal's jaws" snapped shut on the Romans from the sides. About fifty thousand Romans died in the battle. Afterward, Hannibal gathered rings from the aristocratic warriors, and he had a bushel basket full of them.[4]

Hannibal's victories were discouraging for the Romans, but they did not accept defeat; their resolve only hardened. Victor Davis Hanson argued convincingly that the reason was the citizen soldier. Just as the liberty of the Greeks overcame the top-heavy military structure of the Persians, so the "ownership" of the cause by average Romans affected their capacity to continue in a fight. The liberty that was at least functional in Athens in its conflict with the Persians disappeared by the time of Alexander. And the citizen soldier of Rome was not the mainstay of the empire some centuries later. The point is that when these periods of comparative liberty and citizen involvement existed (as they did in Rome at this time), a direct result was an extremely *resilient* fighting force. Facing a military genius like Hannibal, soldiers require that kind of resilience.

In 149 BC Rome declared war on Carthage for the third time. Scipio was a younger Roman officer, who had distinguished himself in the earlier siege of Carthage (which had not gone all that well for the Romans, even though they prevailed). Because of his record, he was made supreme commander despite his young age and undertook a year of fierce fighting, which ended with the defeat of Carthage. At the requirement of the

Senate, in 146 BC Scipio Africanus razed Carthage and sowed it with salt.

Just as the Greeks turned on each other after the Persian threat had been negated, so the Romans turned on each other after Carthage was out of the way. The internecine fighting in Rome at the tail end of the republic set the stage for the empire. The republic was not a time of peace and prosperity, interrupted by the warlike emperors. The time of the republic was the warlike period, and the emperors brought in (comparative) peace. The *Pax Romana* was under the empire, not the republic.

## THE RUBICON AND THE CAESARS

Julius Caesar was a military genius who functioned so well in the old, decaying order that he created the opportunity for an entirely new order. In this he resembled Napoleon Bonaparte, although it might be better to say that Napoleon resembled him. Caesar was young, ambitious, talented, and living at a moment when people wanted forceful leadership more than just about anything else.

The beginning words of his *Gallic Wars* have been drilled into the minds of countless schoolchildren of generations past: "All Gaul is divided into three parts." Julius (100–44 BC) was one of the great figures of world history and the pivotal man in the transition of the republic to the empire. Because he successfully conquered Gaul, he extended the rule of Rome all the way to the Atlantic in the west. As a successful general, he established a triumvirate (a three-man rule) with two others—Marcus Licinius Crassus and Gnaeus Pompeius Magnus. Caesar brought

Britain into the empire with his invasion there in 55 BC. But after the triumvirate fell apart, he found himself in a Mexican standoff with Pompey and the Senate on the other side. He had to make a decision, and his crossing of the Rubicon River with his legions started a civil war from which he emerged victorious. He was then established as the sole dictator of Rome (he never called himself king or emperor). Since that time, "crossing the Rubicon" has referred to making an irrevocable decision.

After Julius Caesar was assassinated (by some conspirators who accurately believed him to be a threat to the old republic), it took some years for Augustus (or Octavian, as he was called then) to establish and consolidate his rule. When he had done so, he became the *princeps* (the head of that locality) in Rome and Italy and *imperator* (commander in chief) everywhere else.

Caesar Augustus was a decent ruler (*comparatively* speaking) who set a number of evil things in motion. He did not live out the ramifications in the same way his heirs did—but he started the downhill slide. He allowed himself many adulteries, but was shamed by similar misbehavior of members of his household.

Nevertheless, unlike many rulers in the ancient world, he knew how to draw some kind of line. For example, under pressure he allowed himself to be worshiped as a god. Some of his successors demanded this honor and exulted in it. But Augustus was embarrassed by it, and when he allowed Caesar worship in Asia Minor, he did it only because he thought it necessary for reasons of state.

After Augustus, moral disorder became more the custom. The rule of law that had been a characteristic of the republic began to erode as each of Caesar's whims assumed the force of law. The perception that the Romans had of themselves governed by law can be seen in the comments of Festus when he was speaking of Paul's case to King Agrippa (Acts 25:16). Whether they lived by it perfectly or not, they believed themselves to be tied to the rule of law in a way that was peculiarly Roman. But as ruler followed ruler, this got harder and harder to maintain. Tiberius was a cruel ruler and a vain one. Caligula was personally cruel and was willing to display that cruelty in public ways: "He frequently had trials by torture held in his presence while he was eating or otherwise enjoying himself; and kept an expert headsman in readiness to decapitate the prisoners brought in from gaol." Nothing like watching someone being tortured to make your meals more pleasant.

Claudius became emperor through a comedy of errors. After Caligula was assassinated, Claudius heard about the murder and hid. A soldier found him behind the curtain, and when he pulled it back, Claudius begged for mercy. Instead of threatening his life, the soldier hailed him as the new emperor.

Following Claudius, Nero was not only a cruel despot but also a vain man who thought he was a rock star. He introduced musical competition into the Olympic Games and entered the competitions himself. And you know what? Son of a gun, he started *winning* them. Of course, he had the power to constrain the judgment of those giving the awards and those watching the performances.

The fact that Rome had vast dominions, immense military power, and staggering wealth could not prevent the realization (to all thoughtful men) that it had become a laughingstock. The empire was run by vindictive glitterati, the rule of hollow men. The stage was set for the arrival of a group that the pagan Romans could not have anticipated, and even if they had, they could not have prepared for that group—the Christians.

## A BRIEF WALK THROUGH OLD ROME

Any modern man, dropped down in the middle of Rome in the days of its imperial splendor, would be dutifully and suitably impressed with the city. The Colosseum, to take just one example, was an early superdome and, like some of ours, it had a retractable canvas roof to keep the heat off. Holding forty-five to fifty thousand people, it was a center for events that you probably never saw in *your* local stadium.[5] They could flood the thing and hold mock naval battles in it.

The Roman Empire was about the size of the United States. When Rome began its ascendancy, some of the cities it ruled, like Antioch and Alexandria, surpassed its architectural glory. Beginning with Augustus, the remodeling and rebuilding started in earnest, and after the infamous fire of Rome in AD 64 (during which Nero reportedly "fiddled"), it was necessary to rebuild almost half the city. That was done on a much more spacious, grand, and artistic scale than what had been there before—which explains in part why suspicion for the fire fell on Nero. It seemed like *his* kind of urban renewal plan. Nevertheless, after the days of the crazy emperors such as Caligula and Nero, each emperor tried to contribute an architectural triumph; Vespasian and Titus built the Colosseum, for example.[6]

During the first centuries of the Christian era, Rome was roughly three miles long and about the same width. The Romans knew how to pack them in, and the population was probably between one and two million people. The streets were so congested that horses and carriages were not allowed. The only way to get across town was to walk or to be carried in a litter. Only the rich could avoid walking.

There were enormous apartment houses called *insulae* (islands). An average street was about fifteen feet across, building to building, and the buildings rose thirty or forty feet high on either side, keeping the street dark. The road was paved, and the impossible alleys veered off who knew where. Some people may *still* be lost in them.

The Romans didn't invent concrete, but they were the first to use it on a large scale. A local volcanic deposit called *pazzolana* made really good concrete, and this meant that huge manpower crews were not necessary to get impressive results, as they had been needed in Egypt. A common practice was to make the building from concrete and then sheath it in marble, tile, or brick.

The narrow sidewalks in front of each building were maintained by the building's owner, and stepping-stones were used in the crosswalks at intersections. This might seem odd at first, but the narrow streets were little more than glorified culverts. After a really big cloudburst, people needed to be able to cross the raging creek.

Little shops were everywhere—bakeries, inexpensive restaurants, produce stands, and whatnot. Because citizens traveled mostly by foot, there was always a need for shops close at hand.

Of course, there were swank establishments for the wealthy—upscale malls are not a recent invention.

## THE ECONOMICS OF EMPIRE

Underneath the glory and splendor of this architecture, the military prowess, and the entertainments—the famous bread and circuses—was a seriously demented economy. Rome, like many previous empires, had conquered a large mass of land and sought to govern what it had conquered. But unlike previous empires, Rome attempted to control everything through an adroit use of money.[7] When it was adroit, things were fine. But as time passed, it was mostly maladroit.

Rome didn't really produce anything. Despite many obvious similarities, this is one of the striking differences between the empire of Rome and the economic hegemony of the United States—as we will see when we get to New York. The United States is a monster of production. Rome conquered other lands, tried to manage their imperial affairs through currency, and imported stuff from these conquered lands. There were many signs of trouble over the years. The army grew as the empire shrank. In fact, the size of the army *doubled* during the third and fourth centuries when there was less for the army to protect.[8] For those who know how governments work, it should not be surprising that the bureaucracy swelled and that a welfare state developed. As the economic woes grew, many reformers attempted to arrest the decline, but every reform seemed to add a new layer of government. Sound familiar?

Diocletian recognized that money was the gasoline for the

car of empire, and he attempted to regulate and govern it—but was unsuccessful. In AD 301 he issued his Edict of Prices, which aimed to freeze all prices and wages. And even in issues that seem to be straightforward spiritual issues, like the persecution of Christians, it is wise to follow the adage to just "follow the money." As Rome grew wealthy by conquering other lands and taking their stuff, so the persecution of Christians added to the state coffers. Diocletian began his vicious decade-long persecution of the church in AD 303.[9]

Similar to Diocletian's financial motives for his assault on the church, Constantine may have had money in mind when he showed support for the Christians and embraced the new faith. Although property confiscated from Christians was a help, there really wasn't that much of it. For *real* money, the pagan temples were endowed beyond belief.[10]

## ROME AND THE CHRISTIAN FAITH

Jesus was born during the reign of Caesar Augustus, and He was crucified during the reign of Tiberius. The famous collisions between the Christians and the Roman civil order are the first of many showdowns between church and state—if we don't count the skirmishes between the Christians and the Jewish establishment in Palestine. It would be easy to represent the relationship as a necessarily hostile one, but that would not be quite accurate. The early Christians were certainly not scofflaws. In fact, their apostles taught them to offer public prayers for kings and all those in authority.

In his letter to the Romans, the apostle Paul described civil magistrates as God's *deacons*, placed there to do the divine will. He wrote that during the time of Nero, soon to prove to be one of history's worst emperors. *He* was supposed to be God's deacon? True, the letter was written in the early part of Nero's reign, the same general time when Seneca the philosopher was Nero's advisor and tutor (AD 54–62), nervously trying to keep his foot on the brake. Seneca was later implicated in a plot to assassinate Nero (AD 65) and was forced to commit ritual suicide.

But even though this demonstrates pagan behavior in the pagan court, the Christians were diligent to pray for their established leaders; they went so far as to make it an integral part of the liturgy and worship. The apostle Paul wrote to Timothy, telling him to teach the Christians to offer "supplications, prayers, intercessions, and thanksgivings . . . for all people, for kings and all who are in high positions, that we may lead a peaceful and quiet life," and the apostle Peter wrote that Christians should "love the brotherhood. Fear God. Honor the emperor."[11]

Karl Marx famously said that religion is the opiate of the masses, and some of these passages from Scripture sound a bit worshipful. But other passages in the Christian Scriptures are not quite so cooperative. In the book of Revelation, the "beast" is seen coming from the "seven mountains," which was shorthand for the seven hills of Rome, and this beast was to persecute the faithful for "forty-two months," which happened to be the length of Nero's persecutions, before he was forced to commit suicide in a coup.

For the city of Rome, AD 69 was a very bad year, a year without parallel. Three emperors in a row died by assassination, suicide, or mob action; armies invaded twice; their temple was destroyed (before the temple in Jerusalem was, under siege at that same time); and the whole empire was racked and convulsed.[12]

The identification of the ruling Roman authorities as "a blaspheming beast" is not exactly a complimentary one, and yet for the Christians it was a very obvious one to make. When the Christians cultivated their open liturgical honor for the emperor, they were not doing so with their eyes closed. We might even say that it was the Christians who first developed the idea of loyal opposition.

The first Roman persecution of the Christians began in AD 64. The Jewish war that erupted just a few years afterward could *easily* have happened some decades before. Caligula, a ruling madman in days when there was stiff competition, ordered a statue of himself to be erected in the temple at Jerusalem. The Roman legate, Petronius, was sent to accomplish this dubious mission. Petronius knew that he was being asked to light a stick of Middle Eastern dynamite. In response to appeals from tens of thousands of Jews, he sent a letter to Rome asking if the emperor was *sure*.[13]

At the same time, Herod Agrippa happened to be in Rome, and he gave a banquet for Caligula. Just as kings do in fairy tales, the emperor was so impressed with the banquet that he asked Agrippa to ask for anything he wanted. No, thanks, I'm just fine, Agrippa said. No, really, I insist, the emperor replied. With that, Agrippa took his life in his hands and asked Caligula to refrain from setting up that statue in Jerusalem.

Surprisingly, the emperor agreed and withdrew the order.

But *then*, the letter from Petronius arrived, which Caligula misread as saying that the Jews were going to fight him over the impasse, and he was infuriated. He wrote back to Petronius threatening to kill him or ordering him to kill himself (a favorite method of emperors). But by the time word reached Petronius, Caligula had been assassinated.

These incidents were the stuff of all the headlines in those days, and it is likely that the apostle Paul had this incident in mind when he wrote to the Christians in Thessalonica that the day would come that the "man of lawlessness is revealed, the son of destruction, who opposes and exalts himself against every so-called god or object of worship, so that he takes his seat in the temple of God, proclaiming himself to be God."[14]

The only way you can read those words without thinking of a first-century Roman emperor is if you don't know your Roman emperors. Caligula had pulled his stunt in AD 39 as part of his program of having his deity recognized throughout the empire. He was not singling out the Jewish temple; he had ordered this action to be performed in *every* temple in the empire. It was an absolute outrage to the Jews, but it was even problematic for many pagans. They didn't mind deifying a king after he was safely dead, but when he acted like a god walking around on the earth in real time, they were extremely uncomfortable. The apostle Paul probably wrote his second letter to the Thessalonians sometime around AD 53, when Caligula's offense was still fresh in people's minds.

Nero was much like Caligula—at least in terms of cruelty, megalomania, and a lot of power at his fingertips. The room was still full of fumes, and Paul knew what would happen when the spark finally came. The Romans previously had a legacy of rule by law, but by this time, they had wandered far off the path.

## CONSTANTINE THE GREAT

Constantine the Great (ca. AD 280–337) is known as the first Christian Roman emperor,[15] but he was not known as a Christian for most of his life. In fact, he delayed baptism until he was on his deathbed.

Constantine was born in what is now Serbia. He first distinguished himself as a warrior in the Egyptian and Persian campaigns during the reign of Diocletian. Diocletian had developed a complicated power-sharing apparatus (a tetrarchy) that helps to explain some historical tangles. In 305, Diocletian and Maximian abdicated (part of the plan). Constantius I Chlorus and Galerius became *Augusti*. Severus and Maximinus II Daia became *Caesars*. Got that?

Sent to Gaul and Britain, Constantine was brought to the front in 306 by his dying father and by his troops. This occurred at York, and since the remains of the Roman basilica there are underneath Yorkminster Cathedral, you might be at the very spot where it happened if you take the tour through the cathedral basement. When Constantius died, Constantine was hailed as Augustus, and Galerius reluctantly recognized him as Caesar. In the meantime, Maxentius was proclaimed Augustus in Rome.[16] The stage for conflict was set. Maxentius, who wanted the throne in the West, rebelled against Constantine and was finally defeated in battle in 312.

There were edicts both before and after the battle at the Milvian Bridge. In 311, the co-emperors Galerius, Constantine, and Licinius had signed the Edict of Toleration, which granted toleration to all religions, including Christianity. Shortly afterward, Galerius died. In the following year, Constantine prevailed over Maxentius in the battle at the Milvian Bridge.[17] Before this battle, Constantine was reputed to have seen in the sky a vision of a cross, together with the inscription "By This Conquer." And so he did.

The battle at the Milvian Bridge left only two emperors standing, in sort of a demolition derby with the ultimate throne as the prize. Licinius was in the East, and Constantine was in the West. In 313, the two signed the Edict of Milan, which made Christianity *a* legal and recognized religion—not the same as making it *the* legal and recognized religion.

It is not surprising that there was tension between Constantine and Licinius. The First Licinian War occurred sometime between 314 and 316. Another war broke out in 324, which Constantine won. In the meantime, between these two wars, there were other exciting events—various wars with the Visigoths, theological rucki (if that is the plural) over various Christian heresies and sects, and the rise of Crispus, Constantine's son.

A driving force in Constantine's life was his desire for unity. He realized this in the civil realm, but was less successful when it came to the church. His desire was that Christianity, which had displayed such ferocious unity in the face of persecution, would lend some of that unity for the civil order. It did, but not in the way Constantine had hoped.

The Council of Nicea, which dealt with the heresy of Arianism (a denial of the deity of Jesus), was convened the year after Constantine consolidated his power against Licinius. In the year after the council, Constantine had his son Crispus executed, along with his wife, Fausta. The details and circumstances surrounding these events are unknown. Whatever it was, it couldn't have been pretty.

In 332, Constantine established a New Rome, the city of Constantinople, a decision that was to have enormous ramifications for the history of the West. He received baptism by the hands of Eusebius of Nicomedia and died in 337. He had given his sons a Christian education, bequeathed enormous amounts for the building of churches, exempted clergy from military and civic duty, established the civil observance of the Lord's Day, and so on. Although he considered himself a Christian emperor, Constantine retained the pagan title *Pontifex Maximus* until the end of his life.

## TRANSITIONAL ROME

Rome has known different kinds of greatness and appears to have gone through the cycle twice. It first rose to prominence in the days of the republic, and its authority was characterized by certain Roman virtues. That was when the capital was collected. In the days of the empire, that capital continued to flow in (by inertia) but was extravagantly squandered as well. Eventually Rome rotted from within, and the barbarians from the north had their run of the place.

The civil order of the Romans was a strange precursor to the influence the Christian church gave to that city. In the early years, the church at Rome was vigorous, dedicated, and valiant. There were many martyrs, and many noble bishops led the church faithfully. Many early popes were genuinely dedicated pastors. This continued to the early years of a recognizable papacy.

For example, Gregory the Great (AD 540–604) established and supported the church in significant ways. Because of the time in which he lived, he had a huge effect not only on the church but the city of Rome and the entire West. In a very real sense, he may be considered the first pope, using that term as we use it today. In another, we may think of him as the last bishop of Rome, using the term *bishop* in the older sense that pertained in the Old Catholic period. Along with Augustine, Jerome, and Ambrose, Gregory is considered one of the four great doctors of the church. He was not an original theologian, nevertheless he was a very capable thinker and consolidator.

Gregory, born to wealth and privilege, was educated for governmental service. He came from an old aristocratic senatorial family that had already produced two bishops of Rome. His early service included his appointment as prefect of Rome in 570, which included presiding over the Roman Senate and administering charity efforts in the city and the defense of the city.[18] He gained a thorough knowledge of business and administration that was to stand him in good stead later.

When his father died, Gregory resigned from all his secular duties and used his wealth to endow seven monasteries, including one dedicated to St. Andrew. Gregory became a monk in his own monastery in 575. He was taken away from a life of con-

templation in 579 when he was called to serve as a deacon
and was sent to Constantinople as papal representative to the
Byzantine court. His experience there taught him that the West
needed to cultivate independence of the East. Returning to
Rome, he became abbot of St. Andrew's monastery and was an
advisor to the pope. He never wanted to leave the monastery,
but was elected pope by popular acclaim in 590.[19] That same
year, bubonic plague broke out in Rome.

The tension between the active and the contemplative life is
a theme in much of his writing. Gregory of *necessity* became
highly involved in secular affairs and began to assume a role that
had previously been held by the Eastern emperor. The Lombards
had invaded Italy, and the emperor would not send an army
against them or negotiate a truce. So Gregory raised his own
army and secured a temporary truce in 592. Later he paid trib-
ute to keep Rome from being sacked, using revenue from papal
lands around the Mediterranean.

The old Roman Empire was dividing down the middle.
The East was to remain intact for another one thousand years,
but the West was suffering.[20] Barbarians were making themselves at home, and the church found itself the only available
integrative entity.

Gregory taught a blend of popular Catholicism of the day
(street-level piety) and Augustinianism (high views of God's sov-
ereignty over all things). He was responsible for the establishment of the doctrine of purgatory, raising it from the level of
opinion to dogma, and he encouraged the veneration of relics
and the use of images in churches. The icons proved controversial, however. At one point, Gregory wrote a letter to Serenus,

bishop of Marseilles, reproaching Serenus for smashing icons that some parishioners were worshiping rather than teaching them that they were essentially visual aids for worshiping an invisible God.[21]

We can see much the same instinct in Gregory's famous controversy with the patriarch of Constantinople, who had begun using the title of universal bishop for himself. To assume such a title, Gregory thought, was to be antichrist. Gregory was not fighting for the right to use the title himself. When the bishop of Alexandria referred to Gregory as "Universal Pope," Gregory refused the title. He claimed that it would puff up vanity and damage Christian charity, which it later most certainly did.

Another contribution should be noted. Gregory once was in the marketplace in Rome and saw English slaves for sale. Asking who they were, the bishop was told that they were Angles (or, as we might say today, Anglos). To this he replied that they were "not Angles, but Angels!" Though this early example of papal humor is unlikely to make us laugh out loud, it resulted in Gregory sending Augustine of Canterbury to evangelize the English. (This Augustine should not be confused with Augustine of Hippo, the great theologian.)

As the center of civil government in the remaining empire migrated east (when Constantine had established the new capital as Constantinople), the importance of Rome was maintained largely by the fact that the bishop of Rome remained there. The five most important bishops in the Roman Empire were (going clockwise) Rome, Constantinople, Antioch, Jerusalem, and Alexandria. All the bishops of these cities were patriarchs in the church at large, but the pope of Rome was considered to be *primus inter pares*—first among equals.

The bishops of Rome began to claim more powers for themselves. At the same time, the cultural divide between East and West was widening. The East spoke Greek and the West spoke Latin, which deepened cultural suspicions and caused real headaches when the church was striving for united creedal agreements and had to work with translations.

Wealth poured into the Western church, and some of the ecclesiastical functionaries got fat and sassy. Tension between West and East culminated in the rupture of AD 1054 when delegates from Rome laid a sentence of excommunication on the altar of the Hagia Sophia, the great church in Constantinople.

The Byzantine Empire, the eastern half of the Roman Empire, endured to the verge of modern times. Constantinople didn't fall to the Turks until AD 1453. Up to that time, *stasis* was the name of the game. In the West, the civil center of the empire had collapsed in the fifth century, and the ad hoc center kept moving around and shifting for the next one thousand years. While it is hard to identify what caused what, the resultant difference between the Christian faith in the East and that in the West cannot be missed. In terms of politics, theology, innovation, and wars, the West was a dynamic and messy place; the East was an orderly place, but it was the order of a museum. The rise of nationalism in the fourteenth century was possible in the West, and the Reformation was possible in the West. The rule of law was a constant necessity, even only as an ideal, but in the East, what is the need for law when you have inertia?

## THE HIGH PAPACY

After the legacy of the republic, the papacy is the second great way that Rome has come to rule the history of the world. The history of the papacy has been a glorious, textured, ribald, romantic, bizarre, heroic, scandalous, and honorable affair. There have been 267 popes and 39 antipopes, depending on who's counting. However you reckon it, the popes have been a major fixture in Western history.[22] It is impossible to understand our history apart from reference to the Roman pontiff. Even to this day, pronouncements by the pope are carried in the media, and Pope Benedict, the current pope, remains a major player in world affairs. Though the political authority claimed by the pope has ebbed in recent generations, he remains relevant. When presidents and prime ministers visit him, it is not just a ceremonial duty.

The papacy has had four major periods. The first period occurred when the bishop of the city of Rome really was *primus inter pares*, the first among equals. He was the bishop of the capital city of the empire, which granted automatic stature to him. Though absolute dates are somewhat arbitrary, one might measure the first period from the second century to the time that Rome went down for the count—the second sack of the city in AD 455. The first sack (AD 410) by Alaric I rattled everybody enough that it inspired Augustine to write his magisterial book, *The City of God*. When the Vandals sacked Rome again a handful of decades later, her citizens saw that Rome in the West was not long for this world. But Edward Gibbon dated the fall of Rome at 476, when the

Germanic leader Odoacer deposed the last emperor ruling from Rome.

The second period began after the second sack of Rome by the barbarians, and civilization in the West found itself on ninety miles of bad road. The pope was sort of an ad hoc political ruler, trying to hold everything together. This period of the papacy lasted to the pope's crowning of Charlemagne as emperor of the Holy Roman Empire on Christmas Day, 800. Before the crowning of Charlemagne, the popes were often the only authorities around, and they had to deal with invading armies and the like. But when the civil authorities began recovering their authority, the pope claimed to be in authority over them, and the pope bestowed on Charlemagne the right to rule as emperor.

The third was the period of papal supremacy when the universal father claimed and exercised authority over the kings of the earth. It lasted from 800 to 1517 when Martin Luther nailed the Ninety-five Theses to the cathedral door in Wittenberg, Germany, and Christendom in the West was divided.

The fourth period is the modern era, from the Reformation (1517) to the present. At first, the pope continued to have the same kind of authority he had before, just not in Protestant lands. But with the rise of secularism, the authority of the papacy declined significantly so that the pope became little more than a denominational head for the world's Catholics. With the role played by Pope John Paul II in the collapse of communism, the papacy has become increasingly influential in world affairs.

In the first period, the Roman bishops were metropolitan bishops with extensive influence. In the second, they had civil authority thrust upon them and did what they could to hold everything together. To be blunt and honest, we owe them a huge debt of gratitude. The fruit of this sacrifice during the dark times, during the aftermath of Rome's collapse, was enormous moral authority, which was then exercised in the third period, after civil authority regained an ability to function and command high respect. This led, unfortunately, to decadence in the papal courts, and the Reformation was a reaction against the excesses of that time. In the last period, many Christians in the West stopped looking to the pope of Rome as their universal father.

The glory of the papacy is in many ways embodied in the basilica of St. Peter's. For the devout Roman Catholic, it shows the greatness of the tradition and church. St. Peter's was built during the Reformation, and the antics of the fund-raiser Tetzel first set Luther off. Luther's protest represented a disgust that ran deep across Europe. This deep-seated disgust with ecclesiastical decadence represented an important sea change in the attitudes of the people, a change that the pope plainly failed to see.

When Luther's Theses reached Rome, the Curia warned that the fuss over the indulgences was just the smoke. But Leo's interest in what was happening north of Rome stopped at Tuscany. Instead of curbing his feckless tax-and-spend habits, the pope ignored the growing protest. Although he could compose clever verses in Latin and Greek, he could not parse the message from Wittenberg Cathedral.[23]

## THE LEGACY OF ROME

One major benefit of empire is the stability it provides. Mail is delivered, products are grown or manufactured, and laws are enforced more or less uniformly. This stability enables people to plan their lives and generally do much better for themselves than they otherwise could have done. Of course, when empires grow, there are corresponding temptations. A strong pressure exists to have the empire retain the forms of the republic while denying the reality of it. Another temptation is that of overweening pride.

During its prime, Rome administered a rough justice, but one that was recognizably justice. And even a critic like Augustine—*after* the conversion of the empire—thought that Rome was far more durable than it appeared from the sack of Rome.[24] That durability came, in part, from the stability provided by the empire. The structure of economic interests made the extension of legal predictability a possibility.

Stability provides certain blessings, but perhaps the later Romans, including the Christians, came to love that stability too much. Consider this overdone language from Eusebius, the early church historian:

His enemy prostrate, the mighty victor Constantine, outstanding in every virtue godliness confers, as well as his son Crispus, a ruler most dear to God and like his father in every way, won back their own eastern provinces and combined the Roman Empire into a single whole, as in former days, bringing it all under their peaceful rule, from the rising sun to the farthest dusk, in a wide circle from north to south. People now lost all fear of their former oppressors and celebrated brilliant festivals—light was everywhere—and men who once were dejected greeted each other with smiling faces and sparkling eyes.[25]

It is easy to compare America to Rome because our country is largely descended from Rome. Historian Michael Grant put it this way:

> With modifications, much of Rome continued to live on within these successor states—language, government, law, Church, literature, art and habits of thinking and living. And of these persistent Roman elements western civilization has remained very conscious ever since, recalling and cherishing them in one revival and renaissance after another. Yet in politics, as in art, the repetitions have never been exact.[26]

Western Europe never really developed a distinct civil identity apart from Rome. Christendom was held together for centuries by the Roman Catholic Church, and in various ways the bits and pieces continued to identify themselves in Roman terms— the Holy Roman Empire. Today a large and growing literature draws comparisons between Rome and America; many uncanny similarities have to do with unmatched military prowess.[27]

But there is a major area where Rome and America are very much unlike each other. The United States produces most of the world's wealth. Rome conquered other lands in order to suck them dry of goods and services (losing most of its wealth as it did so). The United States also uses its military for economic reasons, but the economic purpose appears to be that of opening markets, finding places where we can sell as well as buy. The commodity where our use resembles Rome's the most would be oil. Others have it, we want to use it, and so we do. But even here, we would rather have the mess of drilling located in another part of the world and not in our own backyard, like Alaska. The behavior of the United States toward Germany and Japan after the Second World War was as unlike Rome toward its defeated enemies as can be imagined. We rebuilt those countries, partly from altruism, but also because we wanted places that would compete with us, buy our products, and sell us their products.

Rome was rich, but America is wealthy. The difference is the ability to produce, and the discussion about American empire is accelerating—with people lining up on both sides, agreeing on the fact, but differing over whether it is a good thing.[28]

And one of the central reasons these comparisons are so often made is that we still think of Rome as a place that was stable for centuries, that administered justice over the same period of time, that was technologically advanced (building projects, aqueducts, sewers, and a fleet of merchant ships), and that had a pragmatic can-do attitude. During many periods, that was not the case, but the legacy of justice under the law was nevertheless handed down to us. And this is the reason Americans don't mind (for the most part) being compared to Rome. To the extent that Americans are dominant in the world, Rome is still ruling the world.

M emphis is a great place for blues; Paris, for love in the springtime; and St. Louis, for thin crust pizza. London is our mother of *belles lettres*. Every place is known for something, and some things are more important than others. In this case, literature is one of the ways that London continues to rule the world.

According to Geoffrey of Monmouth, the island was settled by Brutus, a displaced Trojan, who gave his eponymous name to the island. You can still see the *Brut* in *Britain*. According to the story, the island was once inhabited by giants, but when Brutus arrived the place was uninhabited and waiting to be settled. The goddess Diana told Brutus that it would be well suited for his people, and that a line of kings would come from him who would rule the whole earth.[1] The line about the giants helps to explain why giants occupy a significant place in English beanstalkish folklore. Fee, fi, fo, fum, I smell the blood of an *Englishman*.

The Romans conquered the native Britons (who were Celtic), pushing them to the perimeter of the islands. The native populations of Ireland, Scotland, Cornwall, and Wales are therefore deeply connected to the more ancient of the populations there.

When Julius Caesar first invaded the island in the first century BC, the Celts who greeted his troops wore their hair long. They also painted themselves with the juice of a plant that gave them an eerie blue color, and they carried on various other forms of psych ops.[2] But the military discipline of the Romans prevailed over them, and the Romans ruled for some centuries. When the empire started to totter and the Romans finally pulled back, a vacuum was created in the center of the island, which was promptly filled by the Angles, Saxons, and Jutes, who poured in from what is now northern Europe on the Baltic Sea. The aboriginal populations of the islands remained on the periphery.

Various Saxon kingdoms were established, but in the ninth century AD Alfred the Great was the first to unite them into one recognizable kingdom. The Angles, Saxons, and Jutes had been the first wave of invaders from northern Europe, but they were not considered marauders because they were largely taking over for the Romans. They were not the only ones from northern Europe interested in settling there, however. Others followed a few centuries later, generating sharp conflict.

By Alfred's time, the Saxons were Christians and were forced to fight off the subsequent waves of pagan Vikings, the fierce Danes among them.[3] In the meantime, *other* Vikings were making their forays into southern Europe and establishing themselves there. Some of these "northmen," as they were called, settled in France, where the word *Northmen* gradually morphed into *Norman*, and they waited patiently for their crack at England, which came in 1066. During Alfred's time, literature in the vernacular was first established, as a result of Alfred's efforts at education reform. Literary innovation began in England very early.[4]

The unique British character is largely an assimilation of these three strands—the original Celtic influence, the early Christian influence of the Saxons, and then the Vikings who were in France long enough to have become Latinized (and Christianized). This actually accounts for any number of things, including some of the bizarre spellings that still perplex school-children. Take the word *one*, for instance. Where did that *wuh* sound come from? The Romance languages—French, Spanish, Portuguese, Italian, Romanian, and so on—are just deteriorated forms of Latin. Eighty percent of their vocabulary comes directly from Latin. But English is basically a Teutonic language, with large infusions of Latin influences (50 percent of our vocabulary comes from Latin), thanks to the Normans. Part of the genius of English comes from the fact that it is an amalgam with a large vocabulary. As a general rule, our short words are Saxon (*house* from *hus*), and the long ones are Latin (*domicile*).

But because this assimilation has not been undertaken on the grand melting pot scale that has been attempted in America, the distinct strands are still markedly discernible in many ways in the United Kingdom.

## EARLY LONDON

The Romans established London as a town because they needed a place to off-load the ships that made it as far up the Thames as they could go. In other words, the existence of London was only necessary if the island was connected in some significant way to the Continent, which it was under the Romans and then again under the Normans. In this setting, London was ideally suited to be an inland port.[5]

In AD 60–61 the town of London, just twenty years old, was burned to the ground in the famous revolt against the Romans by Queen Boudicea, a Celtic queen of the Iceni tribe.[6] It was a portent of many other times that London was to be burned and has become part of the psychology of the city. In his sweeping biography of London, Peter Ackroyd noted all the burnings: "This is the horizon of the city itself. London burned in 764, 798, 852, 893, 961, 982, 1077, 1087, 1093, 1132, 1136, 1203, 1212, 1220 and 1227. . . . London seems to invite fire and destruction, from the attacks of Boudicea to those of the IRA."[7]

After the Romans left, the town of London remained—kind of.[8] But for a bunch of intermediate Saxons, minding their own business, staying at home, and trying very hard not to be cosmopolitan, the maintenance of London was unimportant. When it was a Roman port, London had a population of about twenty-five thousand people. It largely fell into disuse during the interval between the Romans and the Normans, but was reestablished as a seat of government when the Normans took over.

King Alfred had established what is called the common law in England, but exceptions were found here and there. London was one of them, and its distinctive legal system, separate from the rest of the country, was continued for centuries afterward.[9]

Two grand examples of Norman architecture in London are Westminster Abbey and the Tower of London. Edward the Confessor (ruled 1042–1066) was English on his father's side and Norman on his mother's. He marked the beginning of significant Norman cultural influence, even before the Norman army arrived with William the Conqueror in 1066. He had established a Benedictine abbey on the Isle of Thorn, where most monks spoke and wrote in French. Edward represented heavy Norman influence, while William brought the overt conquest. But because Edward had prepared the way somewhat, when William took over, there was not a sharp break with the past, even though there was clearly an *official* break with the past: "When William conquered England in the year of Edward's death, he carried on the great building work of his cousin the saintly Confessor, and the abbey church contains Edward's shrine."[10]

The Normans made London a defensible place in their construction of the Tower. They were a warlike people, but more refined than the Saxons. They settled in for good and began the process of affecting the English and becoming English themselves. Although William had defeated the Saxons at the battle of Hastings, the city of London still had not fallen. Winston Churchill described William's approach to London:

> When William arrived near London he marched round the city by a circuitous route, isolating it by a belt of cruel desolation. . . . The leading Saxon notables and clergy came meekly to his tent to offer him the crown. . . . Within two years of the conquest Duchess Matilda, who ruled Normandy in William's absence, came across the sea to her coronation at Westminster on Whit Sunday 1068, and later in the year a son, Henry,

symbol and portent of dynastic stability, was born on English soil.[11]

## WYCLIFFE AND CHAUCER

In the centuries prior to the Reformation, the grievances against the pope grew slowly. Various princes all over Europe were beginning to chafe under the authority of the papacy. This rising nationalism is the reason why the Reformers did not die as forgotten martyrs, as a number of their precursors had.

The Reformation should not be thought of as a time when Martin Luther put things a certain way, and a bunch of other people slapped their foreheads and said, "Of course! *Faith!*" Rather, think of Europe as a huge pot slowly coming to a boil. The preconditions for Reformation were everywhere—the heat was spread evenly across the bottom of the pot. When the bubbles first started to appear, they seemed like solitary events— first John Wycliffe . . . then Jan Hus, the Bohemian reformer . . . then Luther. But by the time of Luther, the entire continent was just a moment away from the full boil.

These preconditions were not only theological. There were deep political reasons why certain German princes were willing to protect Luther and why John of Gaunt, a rich and politically influential patron, protected Wycliffe during the course of his life. The results of this protection were a massive theological, cultural, and political upheaval. These same forces were foundational to an explosion of letters—impressive literature in the vernacular language. The Protestants and their forerunners were preeminently people of the Word and hence were people of words.

This characteristic is evident in John Wycliffe and his contemporary Geoffrey Chaucer. Wycliffe was the first to translate the Bible into the English vernacular, and Chaucer was the first national poet of the English vernacular. This shift from Latin to English was profound, and in it many jostling forces were coming together—rising nationalism, distaste for the papacy, and respect for ordinary people. Abraham Lincoln's great phrase "of the people, by the people, and for the people" is actually from Wycliffe.[12]

Wycliffe's Bibles had to be copied by hand and distributed that way. The process was agonizingly slow, but there was a literate market for the Bibles. Wycliffe's followers came to be called Lollards, and it is highly likely that Geoffrey Chaucer was among them. When Wycliffe was summoned to defend his views, John of Gaunt accompanied him. Around the same time, John of Gaunt was also a patron for Chaucer.

Even more striking is the effect of their works on a literary level. Just as we saw the clash between Athenian liberty and Persian control at the battle of Salamis, so we see something similar here in the realm of literature. The Reformation was in large part the result of a rising taste for liberty, and it resulted in more liberty—some would argue too much.

Many Christians, from Chaucer's time to our own, have objected to the bawdiness of some of his works—take *The Miller's Tale*, for example. Chaucer himself came to view some of his writings as being over-the-top and wrote an apology for them. Of course, even a slightly cleaned-up Chaucer would still be rough by modern standards. This really is a matter of shifting cultural mores, as attested by some of Luther's more pungent sayings.

Both Wycliffe and Chaucer were responsible for the creation of a national character for the English in the realm of letters, and liberty is characteristic of both. Russell Kirk noted this fact, quoting G. K. Chesterton:

> Seven centuries after he wrote, the *Canterbury Tales* still informs the world that life is worth living. As G. K. Chesterton comments, "Those strangely fanatical historians, who would darken the whole medieval landscape, have to give up Chaucer in despair; because he is obviously not despairing. His mere voice hailing us from a distance has the abruptness of a startling whistle or halloo, a blast blowing away all their artificially concocted atmosphere of gas and gloom."[13]

When the printing press was invented a century or so later, there was a vast market for the new learning in the common language. Think of the hunger that modern Chinese have for unfettered access to the Internet and you have some idea of the English hunger for the Bible and other works in their own language.

## THE MAN WHO INVENTED MODERN ENGLISH

There had obviously been vernacular English for centuries, but standardized English had to wait until the advent of printed Bibles. And just as Luther's translation of the Bible into German was part of the creation of the German nation, so William Tyndale's translation shaped the English people and the language we use today.

After Elizabeth I died in 1603, the king of Scotland, James VI, was crowned James I of England. He is best known because of his name on the Bible that he commissioned. The original work that established the *idea* of an English translation of the Bible had been pioneered centuries before by John Wycliffe. During the reign of Henry VIII, the whole subject was broached again by the early Protestant William Tyndale. Although he was "just" a translator, his literary genius was without parallel. Many of his coinages are with us today, for example, "Am I my brother's keeper?"; "the salt of the earth"; "the signs of the times"; "they made light of it"; "the spirit is willing but the flesh is weak"; "eat, drink, and be merry"; "clothed and in his right mind"; "a law unto themselves"; and "filthy lucre."[14]

Tyndale died as a martyr in 1536, and his last words were, "Lord, open the king of England's eyes." His prayer was answered in unexpected ways. His work was first picked up in the Geneva Bible, and then, unacknowledged, was quietly incorporated into the official King James Version. Thus did the fruit of his labor come to crown a version of the Bible that is a crown of English letters, read and beloved by millions throughout the English-speaking world over the course of centuries.

Tyndale was one of the few English Reformers who was actually a Lutheran. Born around 1494, he was ordained around 1521. He attended both Oxford and Cambridge and became an outstanding Greek scholar. It is likely that he came under Protestant influences at Cambridge. Influenced by Erasmus and

Luther, he developed a deep commitment to translate the Bible into English. He went to Hamburg, where he studied Hebrew with prominent Jews. Tyndale first tried to get ecclesiastical approval for his translation. When permission was denied, in 1524 Tyndale sailed for the Continent, never to return. His journey was funded by some London merchants. His English New Testament was printed in Worms, Germany, in 1525–26, and of the six thousand copies printed then, only two still survive. In 1534, he believed it was safe to come out of hiding, and he settled in Antwerp, Belgium, and continued his work in ministry. Betrayed by a fellow Englishman, Tyndale was arrested, tried for heresy or treason or both, and convicted. He was strangled and then burned in the prison yard on October 6, 1536.

The *Times* of London said that Tyndale was the "basis of all English language Bibles until the recent fiascos." As such, in many ways we can say he was the father of modern English. Before Tyndale, the only English Bible available was Wycliffe's, and that was only in manuscript form. Further, it was somewhat derivative since it had been translated from the Vulgate, the official Latin translation, and not from the Greek and Hebrew. The Lollards distributed it in a clandestine way, and so the church had banned all unauthorized translations in 1408.

Tyndale was willing to endure great trials because of what he believed about the gospel. C. S. Lewis explained that the "whole purpose of the 'gospel,' for Tyndale, is to deliver us from morality. Thus, paradoxically, the 'puritan' of modern imagination—the cold, gloomy heart, doing as duty what happier and richer souls do without thinking of it—is precisely the enemy which historical Protestantism arose and smote."[15]

Modern prejudices against the Puritans and Reformers make it hard for us to see that sixteenth-century Puritans were not scribblers of fundamentalist screeds, but foremost scholars, poets, historians, and writers.[16] An example on the Continent was Theodore Beza (1519–1605). A friend and associate of John Calvin at Geneva, he was both Calvin's biographer and successor. He first came to fame in Paris's "smart set" as a poet writing erotic poetry in Latin (*Juvenilia* was published in 1548). Also in 1548 an illness turned his thoughts to the necessity of openly embracing the Reformed faith. It is too often assumed that our Reformers were simply hedge preachers or hot gospelers, but that is a gross caricature. In reality, *they were the most cultivated men in Europe.* After throwing in his lot with the Reformation as a preacher, Beza kept his poetic gifts alive by continuing the translation of the Psalms begun by Clement Marot. He also published a drama on the sacrifice of Abraham.

What was true of Europe was doubly true of Britain. The Geneva Bible became enormously influential among learned Britons, and when the King James Version was finally authorized (coming out in 1611), much of the translation was taken over from Geneva, itself indebted to Tyndale.[17] For political reasons, it was important for King James not to acknowledge that he was in effect letting the Puritans get their way, although they very clearly were.

There were certainly destructive elements in King Henry VIII's break with the Church of Rome, the break that established the Church of England. But a number of things were set in motion, far beyond his intent, which resulted in the birth of liberty in the modern world. The birth of this liberty in many ways was tied up with the birth of Henry's daughter, Elizabeth.[18]

## THE GREAT ARMADA

When we consider the plight of small England, facing the array of Philip II of Spain's immense Armada, we should recall the Greeks at Salamis. Many of the same factors were in play— and not just that the victor was vastly outnumbered. The Persians had a centralized command and control system, and when it broke there was no putting it back together. The Spanish filled the role in this drama that the Persians had once occupied. The English were small, scattered, and comparatively disorganized, very much like the Greeks led by the Athenians had been. English liberties that helped win this momentous sea battle were soon matched with a glorious liberty in letters.

After Henry VIII broke with Rome for the sake of his divorce, early Puritans became influential. At Henry's death, his son Edward reigned for a few years and kept the country Protestant. Edward died very young, however, and Mary Tudor, Bloody Mary, ascended the throne. She was a dedicated Roman Catholic, extremely hostile to the Reformation.

Before we go any further, we have to sort out the Marys. Mary of Guise in Scotland ruled there after her husband, James V, died. Mary Stuart, Queen of Scots, succeeded her mother, Mary of Guise. And then in England there was Mary Tudor, the Roman Catholic daughter of Henry VIII and

Catherine of Aragon. Her half sister was Elizabeth, daughter of Henry VIII and Anne Boleyn, who came to the throne a few years later.

As soon as Mary Tudor consolidated her rule, she cracked down on the Protestant leaders, and a number of them were burned at the stake—among them Thomas Cranmer, the archbishop of Canterbury; Hugh Latimer, the bishop of Worcester; and Nicolas Ridley, bishop of Rochester. She also married Philip of Spain, which meant that her ecclesiastical allegiance to Rome was reinforced by the military might of Spain. But she lived only five years after her ascendancy to the throne of England. She died in 1558, and Elizabeth took the throne—and was quickly excommunicated by the pope.

Scotland was a Catholic power, with close ties to France. John Knox was Scottish, but had been part of the Reformation efforts in England under King Edward and had been forced to flee to the Continent under the persecutions of Mary. In 1559, Knox returned to his homeland and was mightily used to bring that nation into the faith of the Reformation. Politically, Elizabeth gained some breathing room to the north as a result. As long as Mary Stuart was alive, though, the Roman Catholics' intrigues were designed to replace Elizabeth with Mary. That did not happen because Mary was later executed for treason. The plan then moved from intrigue to invasion.

By that point, England was crucial to the future of the Reformation. The Reformation had broken out on the Continent, but the political pressures on the Reformed churches there made things difficult. England joined the Reformation late, but the country's involvement in the movement during the reign of

Elizabeth was vital. Whoever the titular head of England would be if the Armada surrendered, he or she would not be a Protestant.

The Armada was simply enormous, and when it sailed, the future of the West was in the balance. The population of England was around four million, and the opposing Catholic powers numbered a hundred million. When it came to the logistical preparation for war, England was hopelessly behind:

> The Armada numbered 130 vessels, great and small, armed, provisioned, and equipped for the service that was expected of it. On board of it were 8,000 sailors; 2,088 galley-slaves, for rowing; 20,000 soldiers, besides many noblemen and gentlemen who served as volunteers; its armour consisted of 2,650 pieces of ordnance; its burden was 60,000 tons. This was an immense tonnage at a time when the English navy consisted of twenty-eight sail.[19]

The ragtag English navy was supplemented with small collections of ships from elsewhere—the City of London contributed thirty ships. Merchant ships were hurriedly converted to be able to fight. Because the professions of peace from Spain had been believed, England had only a few weeks to assemble a militia and build something of a navy. The Spanish had spent years preparing.

As if that were not enough, a vast armed force was assembling in Flanders. The Spanish plan was for the Armada to sail up the Channel to Calais, and there to rendezvous with that great army gathering in Flanders. So a Spanish army was waiting for the invasion across the Channel, expecting to meet the fleet sailing up from the south.

For the superstitious sailors, there were a few bad omens at the outset. As the fleet was sailing north, it got caught in severe storms that scattered the ships. One of the galleons sank, and two others were driven onto the shores of France. Then the second round of troubles for the Spanish began. The English sailed to meet them with a fleet of smaller ships about a third the size. Prevailing winds favored the English, who were consequently able to run up to the Armada in their light ships, pour a broadside into them, and then sail away lightly again. The galleons were heavy, the winds were contrary, and they were so high off the water that they had trouble maneuvering their guns low enough to get at the small English ships. The English were skilled seamen, and the battle started going poorly for the Spanish from the very beginning.

The fierce encounters continued as the Spanish sailed up the Channel. The shores of England were crammed with spectators, watching to see how their little navy would do in their defense. Merchant vessels from all over England hurried to the place. Over the course of days, the Armada sailed farther up-channel toward the rendezvous point with the army in Flanders, and the English fleet followed, harassing them as they went.

The Armada anchored at the rendezvous point, waiting for the army on barges, but it failed to show. One element left out of this grand plan of invasion was the Dutch, who were thoroughly Reformed and hostile to the Catholic powers. When the army was ready to sail, the Dutch (unexpectedly) sealed up its access to the water with their warships. The Armada was anchored tightly together, waiting for the reinforcements that were not going to arrive. At that point, Queen Elizabeth herself suggested a plan, which worked very well.

Eight ships were chosen from the English fleet, loaded up with gunpowder and all kinds of explosive material, and the masts were smeared with pitch. These ships were then cut loose and allowed to drift into the Spanish fleet. As the fire ships burst into flames, the Spanish had two choices—sit tight and burn themselves, or cut their cables and move farther north—which they did.

The next day, the English closed with the Spanish yet again, and the Armada was soundly defeated. The tattered remains of the once proud fleet decided to return home by sailing north to the Orkneys, and then south down the west coast of Scotland and England. As they did, they were pounded by a gale that lasted for eleven days. The defeated fleet became the decimated fleet. One eyewitness described a stretch of beach five miles in length that had eleven hundred dead bodies washed up on it.

Very few ships made it back to Spain. Of the thirty thousand men who had sailed, about a third of them returned. The news was devastating to the entire nation, but especially to the king:

> When at last the terrible fact was fully known, the nation was smitten down by the blow. Philip, stunned and overwhelmed, shut himself up in his closet in the Escorial, and would see no one; a cry of lamentation and woe went up from the kingdom. Hardly was there a noble family in all Spain which had not lost one or more of its members.[20]

A motley navy had defeated the world's superpower, their courage at sea enabled by a series of providential events outside the realm of all coincidence. Queen Elizabeth announced a day of festival, November 29, 1588. All of her subjects were encouraged to go to church and offer thanksgiving to God for their great deliverance.

## THE ELIZABETHAN SUPERNOVA

The reign of Queen Elizabeth I fostered a remarkable flowering of letters and a remarkable convergence of remarkable men. As C. S. Lewis put it, "Somehow or other during the latter part of the sixteenth century Englishmen learned to write."[21] Excellent examples included Edmund Spenser, Sir Philip Sidney, Ben Jonson, and the seventeenth Earl of Oxford, Edward de Vere. Many scholars, including me, believe that this last figure was the author of the plays of William Shakespeare.[22]

Why would he hide his identity? The nobility could go to the theater and enjoy it, but to actually write and produce plays was entirely beneath them. For a nobleman like De Vere to write plays—and acknowledge publicly that he had done so—would be as disgraceful for him as slaughtering his own chickens or making his own candles. It just wasn't *done*. We tend to regard the arts as the ultimate vehicle for self-expression and believe that such self-expression is a primary reason for producing the art. But in the medieval period some of the most glorious things we are still enjoying were produced by anonymous guildsmen.

The arguments about all this can be quite complicated. Suffice it to say that the genius of Shakespeare should be understood as the result of large cultural forces coming together in the education of that aristocracy, and as an example of what happens when classical education and native genius combine to produce this kind of culminating effect rather than a stray bolt of genius striking a random stable hand.

When we come to the explosion of writing in the Elizabethan period, we may consider some preconditions necessary for that to occur. The liberty that contributed to the country's military success spilled over into letters. And the credit for this rising tide of liberty of thought (in England, at any rate) should be given to the early Puritans.

The Puritans are one of the most misunderstood groups in all history. They are usually described in terms that would accurately describe their opponents, and slander is not unknown. The real picture is quite different, *especially* among the first generation of Puritans, the Elizabethan Puritans. The truth claims of the Reformation were formidable, but another factor was involved:

> Many surrendered to, all were influenced by, the dazzling figure of Calvin. . . . The fierce young don, the learned lady, the courtier with intellectual leanings, were likely to be Calvinists. When hard rocks of Predestination outcrop in the flowery soil of the *Arcadia* or the *Faerie Queen*, we are apt to think them anomalous, but we are wrong. The Calvinism is as modish as the shepherds and goddesses.[23]

During this time, the Puritans were *cool.*[24] Their swashbuckling Calvinism, their classical education, and their love of beauty were culturally compelling. Elizabeth was no Puritan, and she viewed them with suspicion. Yet she provided them with inspiration, and they flourished in her reign:

> [Elizabeth I] released their creative power. She was a Queen, not a King, and all that was left of medieval chivalry idealized her into an incarnation of England, a militant heroine inseparable in imagination from the brave, young new nation who was saving herself from those proud old foes, the Papacy, Spain, and France, that had for centuries held her in contempt.[25]

One of our cultural commonplaces is that the Puritans were dour iconoclasts, capable of smashing beautiful things in cathedrals, but incapable of producing anything of literary merit. But if we examine the works produced in the sixteenth and seventeenth centuries by men who were either Puritans or establishment Protestants, what do we find? These men practically *invented* modern English literature: the novel by Daniel Defoe; the cadences of natural dialogue by John Bunyan; epic poetry by John Milton; lyric poetry by John Donne, Andrew Marvell, and George Herbert; and the colossal creativity of Shakespeare.[26] Many times, their contributions are simply ignored, or their standing as representative Protestants is overlooked. One of them, John Bunyan, is acknowledged as a Protestant, but his enormous creativity is often denied by moderns still in the grip of the last creative writing workshop they attended. Bunyan doesn't obey the rules they learned in last week's session. But this is as anachronistic as criticizing the genius who first painted on the walls of the cave at Lascaux, France, because he didn't follow the style of the Hudson River school of painting. As C. S. Lewis demonstrated, the Puritans and the creative humanists were largely the same group of people.[27] Their artistic contributions were almost as striking as our modern abilities of ignoring them.

Even as Elizabeth encouraged this new liberty, she was threatened by it. Under her rule, no Catholics were executed for their religious convictions alone. The men who had overseen the executions of the Protestant martyrs during the reign of Bloody Mary were allowed to retire on pensions; none of them had to flee for their lives. That doesn't mean that her reign was bloodless, but the Catholics who were executed suffered that punishment because of treasonous attempts to overthrow the Crown.

At the same time, many Puritans were well outside Elizabeth's comfort zone, running ahead of her establishment. But she was the reason they were running at all. And the Puritans loved the arts, wore brightly colored clothing, smoked and drank, and loved making love to their wives. They were an *exuberant* group, full of, as the French might say, *les beans*. On the matter of clearing up the standard slander of the Puritans, C. S. Lewis is helpful:

> There is no understanding the period of the Reformation in England until we have grasped the fact that the quarrel between the Puritans and the Papists was not primarily a quarrel between rigorism and indulgence, and that, in so far as it was, the rigorism was on the Roman side. On many questions, and specially in their view of the marriage bed, the Puritans were the indulgent

party; if we may without disrespect so use the name of a great Roman Catholic, a great writer, and a great man, they were much more Chestertonian than their adversaries.[28]

This should not be surprising. If you pull out a map of the world and look at all the countries that have the longest and deepest traditions of liberty, you realize that those nations have a Calvinistic heritage. Various historians have noted this anomaly, but it is not really an anomaly. Those who believe that God predetermines everything are the most likely to think that the king or Congress doesn't predestine anything.

## WESTMINSTER

At the beginning of the seventeenth century, after James I died, he was replaced by Charles I, who was unfortunate enough to be on the losing side of a civil war against Oliver Cromwell's New Model Army, the army of Parliament. Cromwell, a commoner, was nevertheless a military genius.

A common assumption is that two factions were in this terrible civil conflict; in fact, there were *three*. The *Loyalists*, largely Anglican, were with Charles both politically and theologically. The *Independents* were dominant in the army and therefore in Parliament (as controlled by Cromwell) and were against the king in both areas. And the *Presbyterians* were in favor of reforming the Church of England more completely, but were monarchists opposed to the execution of Charles.[29]

During the course of the Civil War, Parliament summoned

the nation's leading theologians to an assembly at Westminster in London. King James had said earlier, "No bishop, no king." The forces of Parliament quite agreed, and since they were at war with the king, they wanted the nation's theologians to establish a common confession for them, along with a standard church polity. "To draft a new church order, an assembly of leading divines was summoned to Westminster. The Presbyterian cause dominated the opening debates among the 121 English clergymen and 30 lay delegates at the Westminster Assembly."[30]

The theologians were charged with creating a Confession and Order for the churches that would establish the Reformed faith in England (and Scotland and Ireland). Because of the Restoration under Charles II, that did not happen. But because the Scots *did* adopt the Confession and Catechisms, the Westminster Standards became the identifying mark of Presbyterians everywhere, and the Scots Presbyterians were profoundly influential in the shaping of the modern world. Arthur Herman argued that the Scots actually invented the modern world.[31] In a sense, the Westminster Assembly invented the Scots who did this remarkable thing. A theological assembly in London wrote a spiritual constitution for the people who were like the kitchen workers at a huge banquet—behind the scenes, making everything possible.

## PLAGUE, FIRE, AND CHRISTOPHER WREN

Between 1500 and 1650, the population of London exploded, transforming it from a market town into a bona fide city. A. N. Wilson marked the growth: "In 1500, there were about 75,000

Londoners. By 1600, there were around 200,000; by 1650, perhaps double that."[32] This increase happened despite significant obstacles. The nation was convulsed with Civil War, the execution of a king, the firm rule of Cromwell, and then the return of the monarchy. To all that, add the Great Plague of 1664–65—spread throughout the city by black rats—which killed about seventy thousand people.

But deliverance from the plague came in a terrible way. The city caught on fire and burned for five days. The city had been burned many other times, but this did not make it any less horrific—only less unexpected. Peter Ackroyd stated:

> There were many representations of the events of those five days of fire. . . . The burning city is severally compared to Rome, to Carthage, to Sodom and to Troy; the classical gods are depicted as wandering through the burning streets, together with Virgil and Jezebel, as the spectacle of flaming London conjures up images of dead or dying civilizations in past ages of the world.[33]

In the aftermath of the fire, a committee was formed to oversee the reconstruction of the city. One committee member was Sir Christopher Wren (1632–1723).[34] He was one of England's bright lights, and he left the imprint of his genius all over London, not to mention places like Oxford and Cambridge. He was a magnificent architect—he designed fifty-three London churches, including his masterpiece, St. Paul's Cathedral. A tragedy of the Second World War was that so many of his churches were destroyed by the German bombing. He also designed imposing secular structures. In addition to his architectural work, he was a designer, an astronomer, a geometer, a member of Parliament, and a founder of the Royal Society (he served a term as its president).

Unlike Nero, the rulers of England did not burn their city in order to build it again. But it burned, and they had an opportunity to build it again. "Within two years of the Fire twelve hundred houses had been completed, and in the following year another sixteen hundred. It was not quite the rapid and vigorous process which some historians have assumed, and for some years London had all the aspects of a ruined city, yet gradually it was rising once again."[35]

## GLORIOUS REVOLUTION

In 1688, England experienced what has been called the Glorious Revolution, or Bloodless Revolution. James II had followed his brother Charles II as king, and his three-year reign was characterized by turmoil. He was the last Roman Catholic king of England, and he believed in absolute monarchy. At the same time, he offered religious liberty to his subjects, a policy that was seen widely as an assault on Protestantism.[36] The established church, the Church of England, discriminated not only against Roman Catholics but also against Dissenters—Protestants not attached to the Church of England. Astonishingly the Dissenters refused the offer of religious liberty from James, preferring instead to keep England Protestant even if it was a Protestantism that made life difficult for them. James was forced out as king, and his son, also a Catholic, was not chosen to succeed him. His daughter Mary, a Protestant married to William III, was established a coruler with William, and the House of Hanover (from Germany) was established on the throne.

This strange series of events set the stage for the independence of the American colonies. The colonies were established by the Crown, and all had their own legislatures. The Glorious Revolution diminished the authority of the Crown, and the authority of Parliament grew to replace it. But the colonies maintained that they had nothing to do with the English Parliament, only with the king. Virginia, for example, had its own legislature, as did England. They happened to share a king, but the legislature of one part of the English empire had no authority over another portion of the empire, any more than the current legislature of South Carolina should be able to pass laws for North Dakota.

The historian Philip Schaff once argued that the greatest act of the Roman Catholic Church was the creation of Protestantism. Likewise, England's greatest achievement—in terms of long-range impact—was the creation of the American colonies and the subsequent creation of the United States by losing those colonies.

## THE PRESBYTERIAN REVOLT

A defining moment in the history of the British Empire, driven by the enthroned folly in London, was the loss of America. The glory days of the British Empire were still before it. But if the administration of George III had not so badly blundered with the colonies and the Americans had stayed loyal to the Crown, what would the British Empire have been like *then*?

Part of the reason the issues were not perceived clearly in England is that the English did not understand the relationship of the whole mess to Scotland. There had been many conflicts between the English and the Scots over the years, but the most significant war between England and Scotland actually began with the Declaration of Independence issued in Philadelphia in 1776. In order to understand Patrick Henry, you have to understand *Braveheart* and vice versa. The rebellion of '45 under Bonnie Prince Charlie ended in 1746—a mere thirty years before hostilities between the Scots-like Americans and the House of Hanover resumed.

Many Scots had settled in Ireland because of land gifts from James I in the seventeenth century. After the Interregnum and rule of Cromwell, Charles II persecuted the Scots viciously during the "killing times."[37] William III brought some relief in 1688, but after his death, more restrictions were placed on them. In response an enormous stream of Scots and Scots-Irish migrated to the colonies, and all of them held a very dim view of the English. And when an enormous stream of Scots began sailing to America, the word *enormous* should not be overlooked:

After the year 1714, their ships began to cross the sea from Ulster in a long unbroken line. For more than sixty years they continued to come. It was the most extensive movement ever made from Europe to America before the modern days of steamships. Often as many as 12,000 came in a single year. . . . In the two years, 1773 and

1774, more than 30,000 came. A body of about 600,000 Scots was thus brought from Ulster and from Scotland to the American colonies, making about one-fourth of our population at the time of the Revolution.[38]

The impact of these immigrants on the development of the South was immense. The War for Independence *and* the War Between the States must be understood as containing an important element of the ongoing conflict between Celtic peoples and the English—up to and including St. Andrew's cross on the Confederate battle flag and the rebel yell. And these immigrants were overwhelmingly Presbyterian.

When war broke out between England and America, Peter Oliver, a Tory writing in 1781, rebuked the "black regiment, the dissenting clergy," for fomenting the Revolution. He was referring to the black robes worn by Presbyterian ministers. When the Americans took up the fight with London, it was not a new war, but the continuation of an old one.

Speaking in the English Parliament about John Witherspoon, Horace Walpole said that cousin America had run off with a Presbyterian parson. At Yorktown, Washington's colonels with one exception were Presbyterian elders. More than half the soldiers in the Continental Army were Presbyterians, and most of the rest were *other* kinds of Calvinists. The British army specially targeted Presbyterian churches because they knew that they were in the thick of it, and the "black regiment" was effective in supporting the war. One name for the war in England was the Presbyterian revolt. One of the biggest controversies in the colonies before the war was whether the king was going to appoint an Anglican archbishop over all the colonies. The rallying cry in the Revolution was "No King but Jesus."

In a letter to home, one American Tory wrote the following: "I fix all the blame for these extraordinary proceedings upon the Presbyterians. They have been the chief and principal instruments in all these flaming measures. They always do and ever will act against government from that restless and turbulent anti-monarchial spirit which has always distinguished them everywhere." The slander aside, it is clear that he fixed the responsibility in the right place.

The historian George Bancroft stated, "The Revolution of 1776, so far as it was affected by religion, was a Presbyterian measure."[39] After the war, George Washington (an Anglican) donated $40,000 to establish a *Presbyterian* college (Washington College). On May 20, 1775, the Mecklenburg Declaration (North Carolina), a declaration of independence from the Crown, was issued. The language of Jefferson's Declaration of Independence clearly depended on the Mecklenburg Declaration, which was the work of twenty-seven oatmeal-eating Calvinists, a third of whom were ruling elders in the Presbyterian church. One Hessian officer, writing home during the war, said, "Call this war by whatever name you may, only call it not an American rebellion; it is nothing more or less than a Scotch Irish Presbyterian rebellion."

The lion's share of the rebel ranks was filled with the Scots and the Scots-Irish.[40] This is not to take away from the contribution made by the others—the Huguenots, the English Puritans, and more. But hordes of Scots had only recently arrived on these shores, with their mistreatment in Ulster and the revolt of Bonnie Prince Charlie fresh in their minds. And so when it came to things British, these Scots were like bears with sore heads. How *many* bears with sore heads? Roughly, in the sixty or so years before the Revolution, about six-hundred thousand of them.

The conflict that led to the American Revolution was fundamentally between the established Anglican Church (in its English form) and the various dissenting churches of America, with the Presbyterians in the leadership position. And even the American Anglicans were much more like their fellow Americans than they were like their fellow Anglicans in England. All the political issues—church government, the meaning of representative government, and so on—were driven by basic doctrinal commitments. This is not to say that the war was over purely religious issues. It is to say that religion in that day was understood in such a way as to permeate all issues much more completely. For us, baptism is a religious issue, and taxation, a political one. But for the colonists (who thought much more "worldviewishly"), these issues were much more integrated. Our take on such things is much more fragmented, which helps explain our consternation over our "culture wars."

America's founders collided with the leaders of England because each side had a well-integrated worldview that encompassed everything. The Scots and Scots-Irish had come to America before the war in the hundreds of thousands. Their political theorists were men like John Locke, Algernon Sidney, Samuel Rutherford, and others. They were eighteenth-century Whigs—and what did that mean? We hope in God.[41]

## THE LEGACY OF LONDON

The blundering of the administration of George III created a
large empire—about two centuries later. In the meantime,
London remained the center of civilization and had its own
empire to build. Still ahead were the defeat of Napoleon and the
establishment of a global empire, and it was really true that
the sun never set on it. The Industrial Revolution took off in the
British Isles first and resulted in a stupendous creation of
wealth. There were growing pains—painted vividly by Charles
Dickens—but the impact of the industrialization of the West
was, taking one thing with another, the means of eliminating
poverty on a scale that previous generations could scarcely have
dreamed of. In a sense, the Industrial Revolution created certain
luxuries, which included the luxury of criticizing the Industrial
Revolution. Dickens was an author who appealed enormously
to the new middle class, a group of people who now had the
privilege of creating the modern phenomenon of the bestseller.[42]

London was an enormous city. In the early nineteenth century, "the first sight of London, the center of world trade, was
an event for even the well-traveled visitor."[43] And by the end of
the Second World War, when the British Empire was little more
than a shell, Harry Truman was still more worried about British
hegemony than he was about the Soviets.

In the Victorian era (1837–1901), in terms of cultural influence and authority, the English people came to the top of their
game. The educational institutions of the later half of the nineteenth century and the early twentieth century—institutions
that produced men like C. S. Lewis and J. R. R. Tolkien—were

in their cultural glory. It is not too soon to say that the likelihood that these two friends will still be read centuries from now is high. But these men were representative in another way. Their generation was thrown into the First World War, the first fully industrialized large-scale war—a meat grinder war. Countless young men, educated in the same rigorous way that Lewis and Tolkien had been, lost their lives.

Every war is composed of countless little disasters for families and individuals. But this was a cultural catastrophe. The old order based on *noblesse oblige* collided with the technological capacity to take away lives, tens of thousands at a time. Young officers armed with nothing more than swagger sticks—conductor's batons, really—led their men over the top into the face of withering machine-gun fire. The old order was staggered, and although the political authority of London remained standing for a time, the city's real legacy after this point would have to be mediated through books. This would include poets such as W. H. Auden; children's writers such as Winnie the Pooh's creator, A. A. Milne; detective writer and classicist, Dorothy Sayers; and stellar comic writers like P. G. Wodehouse. And sometimes gripping histories were written by the men who had made it, like Winston Churchill.

In the aftermath of that terrible war, England walked numbly toward the Second World War. A few men, Winston Churchill among them, saw it coming and tried to warn the nation, but he was not elected prime minister until it was too late to avert the war. And in that setting, if we might reapply what Churchill said of the R.A.F., the English rose to their finest hour. The battle of Britain, as Churchill called it, was a siege both like and unlike the warfare of previous centuries. The battle over the skies of London was a five-year-long ordeal, and as in ages past, fires were everywhere. But unlike the warfare in previous generations, there were enormous bombs and incendiary devices. About one-third of London was leveled.

Hundreds of thousands of children were evacuated during the Blitz—a fact made famous by C. S. Lewis. He put children up at his home in Oxford and memorialized that event in the beginning of *The Lion, the Witch and the Wardrobe*: "Once there were four children whose names were Peter, Susan, Edmund and Lucy. This story is about something that happened to them when they were sent away from London during the war because of the air-raids."[44]

Although England prevailed in the war and the Nazis were defeated, English writer and political thinker Peter Hitchens pointed out that something dramatic happened as a result of *how* that war was won.[45] After the United States entered the war, the massing of American soldiers in England in preparation for the Normandy invasion had a profound psychological impact on the English. They were, during that time, an *occupied* country. Yes, the occupiers were allies and friends, but the American presence nevertheless had a major cultural impact. The English took it in good humor, saying that there were only three problems with the American soldiers—they were "overpaid, oversexed, and over here."

As a result of all this, the English were being prepared to make their most recent cultural contribution—from Rule Britannia to Cool Britannia. The English became acquainted with American music—blues and jazz—and as a consequence, they were open to the early forms of rock. And that set the stage for the British invasion of the 1960s, rockers from the UK bringing American music back to America. It was a significant afterthought.

The reintroduction of the Americans and British to one another—separated, as Winston Churchill once quipped, by a common language—has brought the literary contribution of London into high relief. Just as the Romans, a pragmatic people, looked up to and supported the Greeks aesthetically, so the pragmatic Americans look up to and support the monumental English contributions to literature. Americans have contributed pop culture, technological genius, and colorful slang, but the English still have a way with words. And we know it.

NEW YORK

N ew York is a representative American city (which many cities are), but New York is unique in that it has accomplished this feat by being unlike anything you ever saw. New York is the odd man out and has been since its founding, and yet it has managed to parley this distinctiveness into something that is strangely typical. Not surprisingly, there is a love/hate thing going on with the rest of the country, and even that is part of the story.

## THE $24 DEAL

The origins of many other cities are shrouded in the mists of antiquity and involve mythic heroes, prophecies, wars, and more. The origins of New York, as we know it now, involved a shrewd land deal—a portent of billions of deals to come. The story is a simple one, involving the white man, the native inhabitants, and a small amount of money. "Encapsulated in a sentence, it asserts: the Dutch bought Manhattan from the Indians for twenty-four dollars."[1]

The sale is not registered anywhere, but it probably happened. A Dutch merchant wrote in a letter (1626) that he had just heard from some travelers that the West India Company had purchased the "Island Manhattes" for the sum of sixty guilders.[2] A New York historian converted the amount into dollars in 1846, so that would be twenty-four "1846 dollars." A few years later, another writer asserted that the amount had been paid in "beads, buttons, and other trinkets."

The Indians who lived in the area were called Lenapes (the People). The Indian presence is still with New Yorkers—their trails "followed the high ground to avoid marshes and swamps; they are in use today as our Broadway, Flatbush Avenue, and Kings Highway."[3]

The Europeans began to arrive in 1524.[4] A Florentine explorer named Giovanni da Verrazano, working for the king of France, was the first European to sight and describe the Hudson River. The next year a black Portuguese man, sailing for the Spanish, came to the river. No permanent settlement was established then, however.

Henry Hudson was an Englishman working for the Dutch. In 1609, he sailed up his namesake river and made it all the way to around present-day Albany. On his return trip, he stopped in England, where his maps were confiscated by the English because they did not at all like the fact that he was working for the Dutch. The Dutch returned in 1624 and began to settle in the region. Fort Amsterdam, built in 1626 on the southern tip of what is now Manhattan, quickly became New Amsterdam. A short time later, as Jane Mushabac and Angela Wigan note, a "Danish gentleman, Jonas Bronck, and his Dutch wife [bought] 500 acres from the Indians in what is now the Bronx, named after the Broncks."[5]

The founder of Rhode Island was the famed Roger Williams.

In his biography of Williams, Edwin Gaustad wrote that in 1643 Williams

> traveled to New Amsterdam (later New York City), where he was free to take passage to England. As his ship pulled away from the dock, he witnessed dramatic evidence of the warfare then being waged between the Dutch and the Mohawks. "Mine eyes saw their flames at the Town's end," he later reported, "and the Flights and Hurries of Men, Women, and Children," many of whom were seeking passage back to Holland. Unhappily, among the victims of the Mohawk attack on Long Island were Anne Hutchinson and several of her children, recently removed from Aquidneck Island.[6]

Conflict with the new settlers was present from the beginning. As hard as it is for us to envision Manhattan as part of a frontier, at this point it was.

The English did not show up in force until 1660 when Charles II returned to the throne after the death of Oliver Cromwell.[7] Charles gave everything between the Delaware River and the Connecticut River to his brother James (the future King James II), who was the Duke of *York*. This gift included the Dutch settlement.

In 1664, four English warships showed up and made the Dutch colonists an offer they couldn't refuse—which has been a common business practice in New York ever since. They offered them equal rights with the English and forty-eight hours to think about it. The Dutch were not really in a position to fight because their guns were broken, their supplies in short supply, and their powder damp. And so the Dutch agreed, and the first course out of the American melting pot was served. Fort Amsterdam became Fort James, after James, and New Amsterdam became New York. The settlement reverted briefly to the Dutch in 1673; it was called New Orange for a few months until it became New York again by treaty (1674), and so remained with that name since.

Unlike some American cities that were remarkably homogenous (such as Boston and Baltimore), New York was scrambled from the very beginning. Those jostling together in the early colony were "Dutch, English, Walloon, French Huguenot, German, Danish, Swedish, African, Jewish."[8] Of course, other colonies had immigrants from all over as well, but in New York the phenomenon was characteristically embraced and became part of the cultural expectation. In the 1640s, a "French priest counted no fewer than eighteen languages being spoken on the street in that decade."[9]

Among other things, New York has always been unique. Quintessentially American, it has also been the place where Americans have been able to rub shoulders with people who didn't seem American at all but were nevertheless an essential part of the show. Just as today New York is a large blue dot in the midst of an otherwise red state, so then New York was cosmopolitan when the other settlements on the Eastern seaboard were much more homogenous. The English Puritans had settled New England to their northeast the century before, and in the first part of the eighteenth century, the Scots and Scots-Irish began to arrive and settle in the middle colonies and in the South.

Douglas Kelly remarked on the arrival of that particular homogenous flood, a flood that did *not* overwhelm New York:

> The Puritan movement, which suffered political and mili-
> tary failure in England by 1660, exercised widespread
> influence in the American colonies through large immi-
> grations of English Puritans and later "Scotch-Irish" (or
> "Ulster Scots") and Scots Highland Presbyterians. These
> people did not leave their theology behind, but rather
> brought with them strong views on God, man, and soci-
> ety in general and on church-state relations and indi-
> vidual civil and religious liberty in particular.[10]

New York is unique in part because of who did *not* settle
there, at least in large numbers. In other places, the homogeneity
was strong enough to really assimilate newcomers. Although
much of the famous melting pot immigration came *through* New
York, the city itself has always been more of a mixed salad than a
soup. Each new element has tended to remain distinctively what
it was, set in a new context.

Washington Irving, an early nineteenth-century American
writer, was the one who nicknamed the city Gotham. In their
large history of the story of Gotham, Edwin Burrows and Mike
Wallace comment on some ironies in the nickname:

> In the context of the pieces—mocking commentaries on
> the mores of fashionable New Yorkers—the well-known
> name of Gotham served to underscore their depiction of
> Manhattan as a city of self-important and foolish people.
> Gotham—which in old Anglo-Saxon means "Goat's

Town"—was (and still is) a real village in the English county of Nottinghamshire, not far from Sherwood Forest. But Gotham was also a place of fable.[11]

In addition, it was a place where the townspeople had a reputation for being shrewd. Had it not been for that, the name probably would not have stuck.

## THE BATTLE OF SARATOGA

Sir Edward Creasy had it right. The battle of Saratoga, fought in the fall of 1777, was a Salamis for the New World.[12] New Yorkers were very much involved in the fight against England. In the run-up to the war, "New York had borne the brunt of England's initial policies."[13]

The battle, which occurred in upstate New York, was a high-stakes physical battle in what was really a culture war. The Americans and the English were not just separated by water. At that time in England's history, the leadership of that nation was dissolute. This breakdown likely played a role in the outcome of this particular battle.[14]

Three generals had been dispatched to America—William Howe, who didn't want to go; John Burgoyne, who was vain and far too self-assured; and Henry Clinton, who, according to Horace Walpole, the English wit and parliamentarian, "had no sense at all."

Sir Edmund Creasy summarized it this way: "The war which rent away the North American colonies from England is, of all subjects in history, the most painful for an Englishman to dwell on. It was commenced and carried on by the British ministry in iniquity and folly, and it was concluded in disaster and shame."[15]

The British plan was to have Burgoyne march down the Hudson from Canada, Howe move up from New York, and the two groups meet at Albany in the middle. This would have the effect of dividing the rebellious colonies into two halves, separating New England from the southern colonies. If that campaign had succeeded, things would have gone very badly for the Americans.

Burgoyne in the north had more than seven thousand regulars (half of whom were German), upwards of three thousand Canadians, and a number of Indians. Very foolishly he threatened the Americans that he would unleash the Indians, which was one reason so many from the American militia showed up to fight.

As the British marched south, they captured Ticonderoga, so Burgoyne and his army were in extremely high spirits. They regarded their enemy with utmost contempt. The American as fighter, General James Murray said, was "a very effeminate thing, very unfit for and very impatient of war." But at the final battle of Saratoga, both sides fought valiantly. The Americans prevailed, and the difference was expressed very well by an American named Henry Dearborn, who said, "We . . . had Something more at Stake than fighting for six Pence P*r* Day." We see this theme stretching back to Marathon. The American defenders were not organized from a central command. Soldiers would come and go as they pleased. On the day of battle, an American general would not have any clear idea of how many soldiers he had under his command. And yet, somehow, it worked.

General Horatio Gates had been dispatched to replace the current American general, a man named Philip Schuyler. As the time of battle approached, the militia began to materialize in remarkable numbers. For a long, sustained campaign, the militia could be extraordinarily exasperating. They would sign up for a two-month hitch and then march off on the eve of battle because their time was up. But in their backyard, with stakes like these, militiamen swarmed from everywhere.

Down south in New York, General Howe set off in the wrong direction and captured the militarily unimportant city of Philadelphia. The victory was showy, but beside the point. George III had appointed Lord George (Sackville) as "secretary of state for the American colonies." He was capable of frenzied action at times, and at others an almost unbelievable negligence. His negligence was probably behind Howe's marching off in the wrong direction. "Sackville's conduct in 1777 was extraordinary: after sending orders to Burgoyne to march south, he forgot to make sure that orders to march north were sent to his general in New York City, Sir William Howe."[16]

Burgoyne moved forward, and about four miles from Saratoga, the armies met on the afternoon of September 19. The fighting lasted until sunset. The British held the field at the end of the day, but the spirits of the Americans were greatly raised. They had met the best regular troops in the world and had held their own. It was like a high school football team playing Ohio State and being down by only one touchdown at the end of the third quarter.

Burgoyne was still expecting far more from New York than he was going to get, and he had lost his supply line with Canada.

He had provisions for only a short time, and he needed rein-forcements from the south for supplies, and not just for men. The Indians and Canadians began to desert him, and the American militiamen continued to pour in.

The fighting was concluded by early October, and Burgoyne was soon forced by his lack of provisions to surren-der. The British army was permitted to march to the river, with the full honors of war, and to ground their arms at the com-mand of their own officers. They marched between ranks of Americans who were solemn and engaged in no taunting, mock-ery, or triumph.

At stake was whether the French would enter the conflict. When the messenger arrived in France, where Ben Franklin was, the first question was, "Is Philadelphia taken?" The answer was, "Yes, sir." But when Franklin turned to go into the house, the messenger added the good news. Burgoyne and *his* whole army had been *taken*. The effect, Franklin said later, was "electrical." A treaty was arranged by December and signed in February, in which France acknowledged the independence of the United States of America. If the French had not favored the revolt, in-dependence would not have been achieved, and that would not have occurred without a British loss at the battle of Saratoga.

The British occupied the city of New York throughout the course of the war, which means that there was not a great battle of New York in the War for Independence. John Steele Gordon commented:

New York was occupied by British forces from the fall of 1776 to November 25, 1783 (celebrated as

Evacuation Day in New York for a hundred years). That is the longest period of time in which in a city in the Western world has been held by an occupying power in modern times. During the occupation, two fires had broken out that destroyed half the buildings in Manhattan. The city's population had fallen by half in these years. Many of the city's merchant elite, hopelessly compromised by dealing with the British, evacuated with them.[17]

Although there was no battle *of* New York, it would be fair to identify the battle of Saratoga as the battle *for* New York, a battle that determined the ultimate outcome of the war.

## A CITY COMES OF AGE

In the early nineteenth century, New York was a large town, but it had a number of peers, including Philadelphia. The key decision that vaulted New York to prominence was the decision to build the Erie Canal. In John Steele Gordon's account of America's rise to an "empire of wealth," he noted the importance of that canal:

The Erie Canal . . . turned New York into the greatest boom town the world has ever known. Manhattan's population grew to 202,000 in 1830, 313,000 in 1840, 516,000 in 1850, and 814,000 in 1860. . . . In 1800 about 9 percent of the country's exports passed through the port of New York. By 1860 it was 62 percent, as the city became what the Boston poet and physician Oliver Wendell Holmes (the father of the Supreme Court justice) rather grumpily described as "that tongue that is licking up the cream of commerce and finance of a continent."[18]

These figures are for Manhattan—the surrounding parts of what is now New York City were growing as well. This explosion *was* all due to the Erie Canal.[19] Before the canal, it had taken three weeks at a cost of $120 to move a ton of flour from Buffalo to New York City. After the canal's construction, it took eight days and cost $6. Gordon remarked that, before the canal was even completed, "the *Times* of London saw it coming, writing that year [1822] that the canal would make New York City the 'London of the New World.' The *Times* was right. It was the Erie Canal that gave the Empire State its commercial empire and made New York the nation's imperial city."[20] That was when the position of New York as an economic powerhouse was first firmly established, and the title has yet to be relinquished.

Subsequent developments only reinforced the city's position. The invention of the telegraph provides an example. Money tends to accumulate where the business activity is located, and the telegraph enabled distant traders to start getting in on the New York action. John Steele Gordon wrote:

Once the telegraph made instant communication possible, traders in Philadelphia and elsewhere could operate in the New York market just as easily as they could in their local one, and they immediately began to do so for the simple reason that the best prices, for both buyers and sellers, are always to be had in the largest market . . . New York City became to the United States what London is to the world. Eminent before, this chief metropolis of the seaboard now assumed an absolute financial supremacy. Its alternations of buoyancy and depression produced corresponding perturbations in every state, city, and village in the land.[21]

Empire builders were hauling it in, but out in the street, things were messy for a while. In their history of America, Larry Schweikart and Michael Allen described the conditions in the New York of this time:

A city like New York, despite its advances and refinements, still suffered from problems that would jolt modern Americans. An oppressive stench coming from the thousands of horses, cattle, dogs, cats and other animals that walked the streets pervaded the atmosphere. (By 1850, one estimate put the number of horses alone in New York City at one hundred thousand, defecating at a rate of eighteen pounds a day and urinating some twenty gallons per day, each!)[22]

These were the problems caused by living animals. City officials also had to cope with the problems associated with disposing of the dead ones. But even with the obnoxious elements associated with such boom towns, all those people were there because they believed that it was an improvement over where they had been previously. New York City was overcrowded and had enormous problems. Nobody was forcing people to relocate there. That doesn't mean it was a picnic either—many of the Irish had fled the potato famine of the 1840s in their homeland. Schweikart and Allen continue:

> Like other cities, New York had seen rapid population increases . . . mostly because of immigrants, people Charles Loring Brace called "the Dangerous Classes." Immigrants provided political clout, leapfrogging New York past Boston, Philadelphia, and Baltimore in size, but they also presented a growing problem, especially when it came to housing. . . . When the state legislature investigated the tenements, it concluded that cattle lived better than some New Yorkers.[23]

The American War Between the States occurred in the middle of this century, but New York City had a strangely insular position in that conflict. The city was large enough that when Abraham Lincoln issued an Enrollment Act of Conscription, New York erupted in a three-day riot, involving about fifty thousand men. Many rioters were Irish immigrants who resented being hauled into a war right after they arrived in the U.S. The fact that wealthier citizens could rent a substitute to serve for them didn't help. A substantial number of New Yorkers were Democrats with a low opinion of Lincoln to begin with, and because they were occupied with their own problems, they were not interested in larger crusades.

## NEW YORK RULES FOR BASEBALL

Yankee Stadium was built in the Bronx in 1923. With thousands turned away because of a lack of seats, Babe Ruth hit a three-run homer, and that year the Yankees won their first World Series.[24] As much as baseball fans around the country love to hate the Yankees, New York's dominance in the game is only fitting—the game was invented there. As Bart Giamatti has noted, the myth of Abner Doubleday and Cooperstown was "a legend created at a banquet at Delmonico's in New York City in 1889."[25] The game is an indispensable New York contribution to the culture of America.

Of course, baseball had its antecedents in a game called rounders, but it became *baseball* through a number of white-collar workers who began playing it in earnest in 1842. Burrows and Wallace recounted the story:

> After several years of informal play, Alexander Joy Cartwright, a shipping clerk who later opened a book-store and stationery shop, proposed to his fellows that they constitution themselves the Knickerbocker Base Ball Club. The group—almost all of them businessmen, professionals, or clerks like Cartwright—drew up a constitution and wrote down a set of formal rules for the game.[26]

The variations from place to place included unusual things for us to think about today. For example, what would baseball be like today if the runners ran clockwise? Some people did. But Burrows and Wallace stated, "In June 1846, using the new rules, they took on their first challenger, a group called the New York Club. . . . In the late fifties the game took off."[27] Other varieties were attempted, with Philadelphia and Massachusetts rules, but over time, the New York rules prevailed and a local city game became the national pastime.

Whether the result of organic development or the native genius of the first New Yorkers assembling this game, the elegance of the game is extraordinary. In addition, the game constitutes a remarkable amalgam of what America had been and was becoming. Think for a moment: the game is profoundly agrarian, played on a green field with no time clock and in sync with the rhythms of the season, while at the same time providing satisfaction to the geometric, arithmetic, and industrial mind. The field is laid out with precision—ninety feet between the bases of the diamond, and the pitcher's mound is placed with greater precision. Bart Giamatti explained, "The distance from the pitcher's rubber to the front edge of home plate is fifty-nine feet, one inch. The rubber itself is one inch behind the center of the pitcher's mound."[28]

Baseball was a big city game that successfully tied the cities and the countryside together. America was still largely agrarian, although the cities were exploding. The new trolley lines frequently ended at baseball fields, and people who dashed in front of them were called "dodgers"—hence the Brooklyn Dodgers.

Historian Leroy Ashby noted another interesting feature of the game:

It was, however, the emphasis on statistics that especially aligned baseball with the industrial mindset. . . .

Baseball's statistical dimension was the creation of an English immigrant, Henry Chadwick, who, in 1860, devised the first "box score," a capsule summary that charted the hits, runs, and outs of each player in a game. Soon Chadwick was computing the batting averages and "earned runs" that allowed factual comparisons of players' records. This appeal of statistics resonated perfectly in an era that found truth in quantification. . . . Chadwick shared this faith in the power of statistics to effect beneficial social change: baseball's numbers and uniform standards could inspire "a moral recreation" to counteract urban evils. From Chadwick's perspective, box scores were, thus, nothing less than "mini-morality plays," as Jules Tygiel has written, serving "accountability," efficiency, and the proper distribution of rewards. Before his death in 1908, Chadwick played a pivotal role in transforming baseball from an amateur game into a truly national sport that was big business and featured professional athletes.[29]

As baseball became big business, it continued to attract a certain kind of spectator. The stats were not just a precise way of keeping track of the players; they provided intellectual exercise for the fans.

The players who took the field had all the time in the world—in theory. Unlike the other major sports, which have clock management as a large part of what has to be done, a baseball game, in principle, could last for days. The pitcher can't stall indefinitely, but seventeen foul balls in a row take up time. It is not for nothing that the players run counterclockwise. The whole game is counterclockwise. But baseball is exciting because something might happen at any time.

Baseball is also an industrial game with floor managers, just like in the factories. Every player is accountable. Every player has a batting average and so on. It was the era in which insurance companies began compiling actuarial tables. It was the era in which Frederick Taylor wrote *The Principles of Scientific Management* (1911), where the idea was to maximize the efficiency and productivity of every worker in the factory, keeping track of what everybody did. If one worker fell behind in his widget quota, his manager knew about it right away and could have words with him about his individual performance. Baseball was an industrial game very early in its history, and yet it seems to defy this—floating above the sordid side. It doesn't *look* like a factory.

New York is America's *big* city. And a balancing act has been achieved between that unusual city and the surrounding country, a balancing act for which the national pastime is the perfect metaphor.

## FREE MONEY

The phrase "free money" can be taken two ways. One is "money *for* free," which doesn't generally happen, not even if it is lunch money, and "money that *is* free," which is one of the greatest blessings that can ever come to a people.

As we have considered the five cities in this book, one emerging theme is that of *liberty* and the blessings liberty brings.

In New York, we see the rise of free markets and the productivity that ensues. The United States was the world's first great capitalist power, with New York at the center of that productive dynamo. There were great mercantile powers before this, but capitalism and mercantilism are not the same thing. Both free markets and managed markets have big businesses and stock corporations in them, but they are very different things. New York City today has a gross domestic product greater than the nation of Russia.

The rise of a common understanding of how markets work and the rise of the United States as an economic power have tracked closely together. Adam Smith's work *The Wealth of Nations* came out of the Scottish Enlightenment and was largely applied in this country—but not so much in England. For all kinds of reasons, a tradition of economic liberty took root in America. Though we have had no shortage of officious bureaucrats trying to get mastery over the economy, they have had a much harder time of it here than people in other Western nations have.

One reason was a tradition of frontier individualism, which included even New York City on the eastern seaboard. In a frontier setting, the people are adventurers, entrepreneurs, trappers, scoundrels, farmers, hunters, and other assorted eccentrics. Very few of the early settlers are bureaucrats—*they* come later. But by the time they arrive, a number of generations have experienced the heady draughts of freedom.

In virtually every town in our nation, there are a few people who are one hundred years old. At the time of this writing, they were born in 1909. When one of those individuals was a new-born, he or she could have been placed on the lap of another person, also one hundred years old. That second person would have been born in 1809, when James Madison was president. In other words, *it wasn't that long ago.* You could talk to someone who had been held as a baby by someone who had been held as a baby by James Madison, the man who drafted the United States Constitution. Take it back one more lifetime. That person would have been born in 1709, when Queen Anne was our monarch. Four lifetimes land us in 1609, before New York City was settled as New Amsterdam. Just four lifetimes, placed end to end.

Cities in the western United States that regard themselves as frontier towns have a stronger case—being barely more than one hundred years old. But *all* cities in the United States are, relatively speaking, very young. They are young, and they *act* like it. Part of this exuberance comes from the freedom that necessarily occurs when there are not enough government officials to get ahead of all the entrepreneurs. With five thousand wild bronco entrepreneurs and only six bureaucrats trying to put a bit and bridle on them, it takes a while. And when it does happen, it is usually because some of the more successful entrepreneurs want to keep others from doing the same thing because *that* might bring them the nuisance of additional competition.

But before this happens, there is a delightful pandemonium. For example, the tidy minded think that a given intersection on the north end of town should have only one gas station. That would be efficient and would not be wasteful. And societies that have opted for central planning get one efficient gas station, the only problem being that it doesn't have any gas. The "inefficient" system has four gas stations there, one on each corner, all have gas, and the price is significantly lower than all the efficient places that might have some gas. What makes this work? The results of economic liberty parallel the results of liberty in every other arena of human endeavor—wealth. Joseph Schumpter put it this way: "Queen Elizabeth owned silk stockings. The capitalist achievement does not typically consist in providing more silk stockings for queens, but in bringing them within reach of factory girls."[30]

Here is what happens: a city starts to become prosperous, and immediately government latches on, trying to get a piece of the action, so that it can redistribute "free money" to voters. The inexorable growth of "free money" in this sense starts to drag down that once prosperous economy. Either the industrious go elsewhere, relocating to areas that are willing to welcome them, or they go underground (the black market). Thomas DiLorenzo stated, "The more regulations, controls, taxes, government-run industries, protectionism, and other forms of interventionism that exist, the poorer a country will be."[31]

This accounts for how New York City can still be a center of staggering wealth, which it is, and the municipal government of New York can be in serious financial trouble, which it frequently is. G. Edward Griffin commented on contemporary New York's financial woes:

In 1975, New York City had reached the end of its credit rope. It had borrowed heavily to maintain an extravagant bureaucracy and a miniature welfare state. Congress was told that the public would be jeopardized if city services were curtailed, and that America would be disgraced in the eyes of the world. So Congress authorized additional direct loans up to $2.3 billion, which more than doubled the size of the current debt. The banks continued to receive their interest.[32]

As with many government debts, don't look for everything to be straightened out anytime soon.

The foundations of wealth were established in this country early on. But this wealth attracted managers and handlers who wanted to imitate the poorer European countries that our settlers had just left. DiLorenzo commented again: "Later, from the 1830s to the 1850s, the special business interests who advocated bringing the corrupt European mercantilist system to America supported the American Whig Party, and then they backed the Republican Party. They finally prevailed when, during the War Between the States, all of these policies were finally put into place."[33]

And once a country has become wealthy by one means, the more it seems that this country can (for a time) do things that will eventually end in poverty. This is not immediately obvious, but it will become obvious to everyone at some point. When the prodigal son ran off and started buying drinks on the house for everyone, he did not run out of money on the first day. But a day of reckoning was coming regardless. In a similar way, when nations that were once on the top of the world wake up one day to find out this is no longer the case, it is usually too late at that point to do anything about it. Countries that are staggeringly wealthy can afford to be profligate for a time, and they think they can "afford" the drag on the economy such interference creates. But one thing leads to another, and pretty soon all eight pistons are gummed up—if you are fortunate enough to still have a car with eight pistons.

New York City may one day succeed in chasing all entrepreneurs from the city through more fees and taxes that will be advertised as a way to make the wealthy pay their "fair share." If that happens, the results are not likely to be a good outcome, least of all for low-income citizens.

## SCRAPING THE SKY

New York is well known for building into the stratosphere. Although the Empire State Building was constructed in the midst of the Great Depression, it was completed ahead of time and under budget.[34] The Empire State Building would serve as the world's tallest building for the next forty years, impressing that fact on the minds of schoolchildren everywhere.

The Chrysler Building, completed the same year, is a striking example of the Art Deco style and is a *beautiful* building. Since that time, cities around the nation have gone in more for glass shoeboxes, set on one end, giving birds something to fly into, but skyscrapers used to be architectural statements worth listening to. Jane Holtz Kay described them well: "In Manhattan, the Art Deco skyscrapers soared, their height transforming them into urban mountains. Their stepped-back shapes, dictated by Manhattan's ordinance of 1919 to let in light, created a new skyline and streetscape that bestirred civic pride."[35]

A generation earlier, another technological triumph in New York had been the building of the Brooklyn Bridge. Completed in 1883, the bridge took fourteen years to construct, and it succeeded in joining the first and third most populated cities (Manhattan and Brooklyn) in the United States. These cities were typically connected by water, but when the temperature dropped below freezing, it was incredibly difficult to travel between them. The bridge was one of the wonders of the world at that time, a long suspension bridge extending more than a mile from end to end, and the twin towers of the bridge dominating the skyline.

Skyscrapers began to arrive with the Flatiron Building (1902) and the Times Building (1904). The move of the *New York Times* to Longacre Square helped to establish that place, now renamed Times Square, as the center of the city, and in some senses the center of the world.

The city of New York was busy building up into the sky, across the water, and down into the earth. The subway system was constructed during the first thirty years of the twentieth century.[36] Although steam shovels were available, thirty thousand men had to dig by hand because of all the wire and conduit that had already been buried.

The infrastructure of New York City, which today seems like such a given to us, was built over many years. A child growing up in New York today might be forgiven for believing that it was steel and concrete "all the way down," but it was a city that was *built.*


## TERRORISM AND COMMERCE

On September 11, 2001, two airliners were flown into the Twin Towers of Manhattan, and both buildings were completely destroyed, taking three thousand souls with them. Another plane struck the Pentagon in Washington, D.C., and a fourth airliner crashed in the fields of Pennsylvania. New York, along with the world, was ushered into a new era.

The World Trade Towers were the world *trade* towers. Selected by certain fanatics because of their role in the increasing globalization of world economies, the towers had to come down. They symbolized the economic hegemony of the West and were hated and resented by fundamentalist Muslims. The towers were at the center of a New York economy that was in its turn at the center of America's economy, which in its turn is the central economy in the world. As an attack on the world's economic system, the hit has to be considered a bull's-eye.

It is difficult for us to understand this now, but for many centuries, the Muslim powers were at the *center* of civilization, and they scarcely paid any attention to the scattered Christian nations to their northwest. Embedded deeply in today's Muslim psyche is the notion that something has gone terribly wrong— Muslims have been dislodged from their position of preeminence, and many of them therefore intend to return to a robust obedience of the Koran so that Allah will be pleased to restore the rightful order of Islamic dominance, the way things once were and the way things are supposed to be.[37]

Five hundred years of Christian ascendancy have been more than a little exasperating for them, and with the explosion of Western wealth in the last generation the whole thing has grown to ridiculous proportions. At the same time, globalization (and the communication system that supports it) has resulted in ordinary folks on the street actually *knowing* how wealthy the West is. In 1900, very few individuals in the Muslim world would have been able to visit the West or see anything of how Westerners live through television and the movies. That has all changed, and consequently the disparity and the troubling questions it generates are obvious to all—and there is no better representation of Western success than New York, which made the city a fat target to make a point.

## THE LEGACY OF NEW YORK

New York City is too close for us to see accurately. Future historians will have the necessary detachment, but they won't have the living, breathing contact with New York—just as we do not have direct connection to ancient Jerusalem or medieval London.

Yet even though we are very close, we can tell that New York City is built on money, and it has been this way from the beginning. John Steele Gordon remarked that the Dutch established the tone for the city that would last: "While the Dutch ruled on the Hudson for only forty years, they left a deep impress on the city they founded. It is still, nearly 350 years after the English seized it in 1664, the most commercially minded great city in the world."[38]

As an up-and-comer, New York was commercially minded from the start, but did not occupy the position of preeminence until it was 250 years old. And that, if you stop to think about it, is remarkably young. Founded in the early part of the seventeenth century, New York was the world's financial center by the end of the nineteenth century. In his history of money, Jack Weatherford described how New York came of age:

During the latter years of the nineteenth century, New York began to replace London as the world financial center. The center had slowly worked its way from ancient Lydia across Greece and Rome, through Renaissance Florence, and then on to London during the early industrial era. Gradually, in the decades after the American Civil War, the financial center shifted from the Old World to the New.[39]

Comparisons between the wealth of Rome and the wealth of America are common. But Rome had this position of authority for centuries and was not very flexible. Given the nature of the case, Rome did not need to be. But America, with New York at the center, is nothing if not flexible. Cullen Murphy commented on the source of this flexibility:

America does possess one quality that Rome didn't have at all. Rome's elites were deeply satisfied with their lot, their station, their state of mind. Their motto might have been "*Nihil potest ultra*"—a phrase from Cicero that Madison Avenue would render as "It doesn't get any better than this." Americans would glare in disbelief at Rome's self-satisfaction. . . . Rome's economy was the same at the beginning as it was at the end: agrarian, Iron Age, preindustrial. America has lived through more social transformation in a few centuries than Rome did in a millennium. . . . Rome dissolved into history, successfully but only once. America has done so again and again.[40]

So is America an empire? Niall Ferguson said *yes*, but with a twist: "Officially, to be sure, the United States remains an empire in denial."[41] It is not an empire in the traditional sense, but the economic power that is being wielded is enormous and growing.

Going forward, America is likely to become an obvious empire, with New York at the financial center. On its own, that is no great cause for alarm, but to the extent that America starts capitulating to the temptations of empire, Americans should care about these issues a lot more than we appear to.

Fortunately, certain restraints remain in place. The Constitution forbids the president from toppling sovereign states on his own authority as *imperator*, a convention that is still honored. But elsewhere, things have come unstuck. The founding father most interested in centralization was Alexander Hamilton, and if we were to take him on a three-day tour of New York City, *he* would not be able to comprehend the transformations that have taken place.

But as common as it has become to cast the United States as the new Rome, one striking difference remains. Rome conquered other lands and then imported stuff from them. Italy did not become a manufacturing center—just the reverse. But the United States is a monster of *production.* Advocates of American empire want trade. We have an awful lot to trade and, for the foreseeable future, the bulk of those deals will probably come together in New York.

The problems we are facing during the course of the next century appear to be intractable in many ways. The basic tensions and difficulties cannot be altered by anything as simple as a change of policy or the election of this president or that one. New York City is at the center of a fabulously wealthy collection of nations, and short of an asteroid landing on Manhattan, this is not going to change anytime soon. The legacy of New York is the wealth that free trade brings, and if we want to keep that legacy, we have to learn how to handle that wealth. Man does not live by bread alone, and this is not altered by adopting *hattan* as a suffix.

EPILOGUE

As we take a few minutes to look back over our shoulders at these five cities, we ought to consider a few more things. Rudyard Kipling wrote many lines that have made it into the common parlance, and one of them comes from "The Ballad of East and West":

> Oh, East is East, and West is West, and never the
>     twain shall meet,
> Till Earth and Sky stand presently at God's great
>     Judgment Seat . . .

Many feel the same way about other dualities, but *particularly* about the distinction between the City of God and the city of man. It is assumed that Augustine, who gave us this formulation, was talking about earthly stuff on the one hand and the things of God, entirely heavenly and spiritual, on the other— and never the twain shall meet. Bringing up the City of God and the city of man is assumed to be dragging religion into the discussion. One is religious and one is secular, and "never the twain shall meet," or so the thinking goes.

But this is far too facile, and this notion neglects to take into account something that happened just a few miles outside the city of Jerusalem, and that is the birth of Jesus Christ. Jesus of Nazareth was born into *this* world and had a hometown here, and that hometown was nearer to some big cities than to others. When His folks went "to the city," it was one city and not others.

On top of all this, He commanded His disciples to go out into the world and preach the gospel to all the nations, baptizing and discipling them (Matt. 28:18–20). The apostles interpreted this command, quite rightly, as involving the great cities of their day; consequently, preaching in the great cities of their day was at the very center of their strategy.

Yet there is far more than this. God knew that He was going to send these men out in this way, and He did a number of things to prepare the nations for the message that was coming to them. One thing He did was to make the pagan nations restless in their bondage, unhappy with their condition of slavery. It is therefore not surprising when we see that Paul taught clearly that the Holy Spirit of God is *the Spirit of liberty*. He said, "Now the Lord is the Spirit, and where the Spirit of the Lord is, there is freedom" (2 Cor. 3:17 ESV). The Lord saw His ministry, a ministry of liberation, explicitly in these terms:

> The Spirit of the Lord is upon me,
>     because he has anointed me
>     to proclaim good news to the poor.
> He has sent me to proclaim liberty to the captives
>     and recovering of sight to the blind,
>     to set at liberty those who are oppressed. (Luke
>     4:18 ESV)

This is a quotation from the prophet Isaiah, given with slightly different wording. The incarnation of God's Word in Jesus was God's declaration of unlimited Jubilee (Isa. 61:1). It was a prophecy of the coming days of the Messiah, and Christ clearly saw Himself as the fulfillment of this prophetic word. The incarnation meant that freedom came *here*, down to us, and it did not mean that freedom was offered to us somewhere far off, beyond the clouds. Because of the incarnation, Christians have been taught to prary for Christ's kingdom to *come*, not for His kingdom to *go*. Jesus taught in that prayer that Christians are supposed to pray God's will would be done *on earth* as it is done in heaven. This is not the same as praying that God's will be done in heaven if and when they eventually get there.

And though the Spirit empowered the apostles as they preached their message, anointing it, there are also clear indications that the Spirit was at work among the heathen nations, preparing them long before the apostles got there. Before the ministers of Christ arrived with the gospel, preparations were being made for the reception of that gospel. We saw one stark example with the counsel of Epimenides to the Athenians, resulting in their worshiping the "unknown god." But we also have evidence of God working among them generally:

> He made from one man every nation of mankind to live on all the face of the earth, having determined allotted periods and the boundaries of their dwelling place, *that they should seek God, in the hope that they might feel their way toward him and find him.* Yet he is actually *not far* from each one of us, for "In him we live and move and

have our being"; as even some of your own poets have said, "For we are indeed his offspring." *Being then God's offspring,* we ought not to think that the divine being is like gold or silver or stone, an image formed by the art and imagination of man. The times of ignorance God overlooked, but now he commands all people everywhere to repent, because he has fixed a day on which he will judge the world in righteousness by a man whom he has appointed; and of this he has given assurance to all by raising him from the dead. (Acts 17:26–31 ESV, emphasis added)

The apostle cut no slack for the idolatry itself, and he said that it was a corruption of what God had been offering them in His natural revelation. At the same time, he indicated God's patience with them—"the times of ignorance God overlooked"—and stated plainly that God *was* working with them. What are some indications of that work?

We don't want to reverse terms glibly, but there *is* a sense in which we can say that where the Spirit is, there is also freedom, and we can also say that wherever liberty starts to emerge (even if only as an unattained ideal), there also the Spirit of the Lord is at work. In all these cities, even in their times of darkness (and there have been many such periods), we have been able to discern the approach of this second city, this heavenly city. This city is the mother of all who believe, Paul argued, and he said specifically that this mother is a *free* woman. Her children are not slaves, but free: "The Jerusalem above is free, and she is our mother" (Gal. 4:26 ESV).

Each of these cities has seen, and been the recipient of, significant developments in the idea of liberty. The development of what we call the West has been the development of individual and corporate cultural liberty. The reasons have frequently been misunderstood, and the thanks for the blessings it has brought have been frequently misattributed to one false god or another. But it is a fact nonetheless. Painting with a broad brush, Jerusalem represents the soul set free. Athens established the ideal of free inquiry. Rome passed on to us liberty of movement, liberty under law. London was the place where the literary imagination was set free. And New York, with its commercial success, has shown us freedom to trade, and the subsequent freedom from want. Of course, these are not watertight compartments, and a host of qualifications apply.

There is something about freedom we have to understand. The point is not that liberty or freedom produces good results inexorably and universally, as though all those results were perfect ball bearings being manufactured in the factory of God. Freedom produces, among other things, countless screwups, mistakes, rebellions, apostasies, and more. Freedom is *messy* and presents a standing affront to the tidy minded. But historian Christopher Dawson once said that the church lives in the light of eternity and can afford to be *patient*. Robert E. Lee, with penetrating wisdom, put it this way: "The work of progress is so immense and our means of aiding it so feeble; the life of humanity is so long, that of the individual so brief, that we often see only the ebb of the advancing ways, and are thus discouraged. It is history that teaches us to hope."[1]

By taking the long view (viewing history in segments of five hundred years or so), things look better than they do if we take it in five-year segments or, depending on the president, four-year segments. The development of liberty in the world was not launched in a certain year, taking off like the space shuttle. Rather, it is like hiking up a long, gradual slope toward the peak of a distant mountain, with many valleys, crevices, and gulches in between. It is necessary to step back and look at the big picture of what's happening, which frequently includes thirty yards forward and twenty yards back.

When liberty arrives, all kinds of things start to happen— many of them bad. But one of the comforting things is that in the long run, stupidity doesn't work. We learn our lessons slowly. Give us a few centuries, and we have one small part of it down. As the ramifications of liberty unfold, there are those who see (and often see accurately) the destructive power of abused liberty, and they are not hesitant to warn us. With freedom of speech come gossip and slander. With freedom of the press comes pornography. With freedom of markets come greed and acquisitiveness. And so on. It is *very* easy to see the glass half empty. But at the same time, the glass is half full.

In his famous appeal for liberty of the press, John Milton wrote these words:

What a collusion is this, whenas we are exhorted by the wise man to use diligence, "to seek for wisdom as for hidden treasures" early and late, that another order shall enjoin us to know nothing but by statute! When a man hath been laboring the hardest labor in the deep mines of knowledge, hath furnished out his findings in all their equipage, drawn forth his reasons as it were a battle ranged, scattered and defeated all objections in his way, calls out his adversary into the plain, offers him the advantage of wind and sun, if he please, only that he may try the matter by dint of argument; for his opponents then to skulk, to lay ambushments, to keep a narrow bridge of licensing where the challenger should pass, though it be valor enough in soldiership, is but weakness and cowardice in the wars of Truth. For who knows not that Truth is strong next to the Almighty?[2]

Milton's argument is simple and, kept within reasonable bounds, compelling. First, deal with the obvious—restriction and compulsion are inescapable. Given the nature of the world, *somebody* is going to have to accept restrictions on whatever it was he wanted to do. The subtitle of Milton's pamphlet is "A Speech for the Liberty of Unlicensed Printing, To the Parliament of England." He was arguing for freedom of the press not because everything printed must necessarily be true, but because truth and error will get sorted out in the long run, and probably much quicker if we just let it rip rather than try to *manage* the whole process. Somehow the managers of the process are frequently found to be an essential part of the problem, and it turns out they tend to manage the discussions in such a way that *that* interesting fact never comes out.

Milton was not an anarchist. Nor did he believe in no restrictions. On the contrary, his argument was *for* a fundamental restriction—a restriction on the governing authorities. He proposed that their license to license printing be revoked. He wanted to take that license away. A similar mentality lies under-neath the American Bill of Rights. As originally conceived, the Bill of Rights restricted what the federal government could do. "*Congress* shall make no law . . ."

So Jerusalem is a great and standing metaphor for spiritual liberty. God has worked in Jerusalem for centuries, making this point in countless ways. But frequently that meant the inhabi-tants of Jerusalem were identified with the inhabitants of Sodom, and the name of their city was taken away from them and used in the image of a *New* Jerusalem. The name *Jerusalem* represents spiritual liberty, in part because we now know that we cannot just take that name and use it as a religious talisman. God wants our freedom from sin to go deeper than that; or to change the image to the Jerusalem above, He wants our freedom from sin to go higher than that.

Jesus taught plainly that anyone who heard His words and did them was building his house on the rock. Those who heard His teachings and did not take them to heart were like the one who built his house on sand (Matt. 7:24–27). When Jesus spoke these words, the house of the Lord, the temple of the Lord that Herod was building, was still under construction. The Jews were still in the midst of a huge project, building the house of the Lord on the rock of Mount Moriah. That rock, as a physical rock, is still there today, as countless pilgrims can attest. But the words of Jesus are the true Rock, just as *He* is the true Rock, the Stone the builders rejected.[3]

Jesus was warning them about an impending storm—the Roman armies would besiege Jerusalem within a generation, and the temple they were building, their house of God, would not be able to stand, precisely because they had not grounded their work on obedience to the words of Jesus. Their house, built on an imposing *physical* rock, was actually built on spiritual sand. The importance of Jerusalem is that we learn from it that Jerusalem is unimportant. What matters is keeping God's commands in love, and the central command is to trust Him. When the gospel of God's grace liberates us from our sin and absorption with self, it connects naturally and readily to every other form of liberty.

Athens began experimenting with democracy, and the citizens soon discovered the limitations of that system. As Winston Churchill famously put it, democracy is the worst form of government, except for all the others. But in that process, they discovered (in fits and starts) that free men fight better than do slaves. They also discovered that the free exchange of ideas allows the strengths and weaknesses of each idea to be probed and examined.

As with every other form of freedom, this has been radically misunderstood and misapplied. For some, academic freedom is just a fancy name for intellectual relativism. But this is self-refuting—if there is no truth, and all ideas are relative, academic freedom (itself an idea) is relative and can be abandoned as soon as someone pays us enough to abandon it or threatens us sufficiently. When Milton called for the untrammeled exchange of ideas, he fully expected truth to come out ahead in any collisions. He was no relativist.

That numerous people misunderstand intellectual liberty does not prevent the fruit of intellectual liberty from manifesting itself over time. Chesterton said the purpose of an open mind is the same as that of an open mouth—it is meant to close on something. Being perpetually open to all truth is indistinguishable from being closed to all truth. Unless truth is *grasped*, what good is it?

Intellectual liberty cannot be prized on the ground that all ideas are equally worthless or equally unattainable. Fortunately, in the free footrace of all ideas, all forms of relativism are on the sidelines, sucking wind after the first lap. We are grateful to Athens, not for every idea to come out of Athens, but for the freedom to reject most or all of them.

Rome gave us a widespread understanding of the civic liberty that becomes possible when we submit to the confines of equitable laws. Form and freedom are difficult to maintain together, and Rome certainly had centuries when it did not do so—both under the pagan emperors and under a compromised papacy. But even when Rome failed to maintain the standard it had set, the standard remained set. The apostle Paul did not hesitate to use the Roman system of appeals, and he urged the burgeoning Christian movement to honor the existing authorities. The authorities had to be resisted when they claimed the mantle of God, but until that point, their service was honorable, noble, and God-given.

Reasonable laws, enforced in an even-handed spirit of justice, make life predictable. When life is not predictable, it is not long before people stop trying to predict it, and they live for today. And when that happens, life deteriorates to the squalid level of subsistence living, hand to mouth.

London set free the literary imagination. Since there is money in books, that process has been picked up by New York, but London was responsible for placing extraordinary literature in the hands of ordinary people. When Milton argued that Parliament should allow an unlicensed press, he was arguing, ultimately, for the liberation of the imagination.

We often misunderstand the classics. They are not the books that the ancients produced, to be compared (to our shame) to the average supermarket romance novel of today. No, the ancients produced plenty of garbage, just as we have. But *their* garbage has not lasted to the present. We don't know about it—just as five hundred years from now, nobody will be reading our garbage. Why would anyone save the garbage?

Having just emerged from the twentieth century, we are still aware that literary sensations, novelistic fads, hot authors for a fortnight, and Book-of-the-Month pan-flashers are within living memory. But which authors from this last century will find readers five hundred years from now? Will *any*? I suspect so, but I also suspect that most of them will be Christians—and I offer the names of J. R. R. Tolkien, C. S. Lewis, T. S. Eliot, and G. K. Chesterton. And this means that wide-eyed schoolchildren will be reading these books, amazed and delighted, and will be tempted to think of the twentieth century as a golden age of literature.

And in one sense it was, and London was the reason. Not only did London publish many of these works (New York being the place where the American editions were published), but it also has to be said that London was the center of a culture that produced some of the finest imaginative minds Christendom has produced thus far. We have traced the beginnings to the reign of Queen Elizabeth I, but the fruition came in the present day, in the reign of Queen Elizabeth II.

New York is familiar to all of us and as a result we may not look at it closely enough. It would be a useful exercise for you to turn to the notes in this book. Where were most of the books published? Overwhelmingly, the books that constitute the vocabulary of our minds are published in New York, with London coming in second. As discussed earlier, this is due to any number of factors, but the fact remains that New York is the central engine in the economy of the West. We should remember freedom does not mean that everything that results from it is good, true, and beautiful. Quite a bit of it is bad, false, and ugly. But what is worthless rarely finds a long-term use.

And what is worthwhile likely has some important connection to New York. A few years ago, a popular game of finding "six degrees of separation" between any given person and a particular celebrity was making the rounds. If we were to play the same game with any object in the room where you are now sitting and New York City, we are probably talking about one or two degrees of separation. In the room where I am typing this, I am surrounded by books, most of which came to me from New York. The rest of them probably have a tight connection to New York somehow, whether through the shipping of paper, the processing of financial accounts, or the advertising that enabled me to find out the book existed.

Wherever we are, we can see objects that were made in a factory somewhere. Whether we are talking about a computer monitor, a book jacket, a CD for the computer, a salt shaker, a table, the handles on the kitchen cabinets, the alternator in the car, or your toddler's rattle toy, the chances are outstanding that it was made in, went through, or was financed by New York.

When people ask God for their daily bread, as He instructs in His Word, and as He liberally gives to them accordingly, they should also thank Him for the role of that particular city.

This can all seem fairly tension-ridden and more than a little untidy. The English theologian N. T. Wright has commented insightfully on the messy nature of God's work in the world and the gracious nature of His intervention:

> The Creator God desired to work within his own world in order to heal it. No solution imposed from a great height would have sufficed. That would have resulted only in the obliteration of the world by a sweeping declaration of justice, or a totally unjustifiable and immoral wiping of the slate clean in a display of sentimental mercy, with God declaring that humanity's wrong choices didn't really matter, human freedom wasn't really significant, and that all along these human creatures had been puppets, whose strings he could pick up and tweak back into obedience any time he chose. He was therefore bound to work the salvation of the world *from within*; and that meant operating within tension and ambiguity.[4]

In place after place, the Scriptures speak of God transforming the city of man from within. Put crudely, the City of God is invasive, and as new centers of worship are established, replacing all the old altars, the character of the city of man is gradually transformed. It does not happen overnight, but it does happen. Jesus compared it to the growth of leaven within a loaf of bread.

He compared it to a small mustard seed, growing up into a large plant, where birds could build their nests. The prophet Daniel saw the interpretation of the king's dream. Nebuchadnezzar had seen a great statue, made of different precious metals. But the statue was struck and destroyed by a mysterious object: "The stone that struck the image became a great mountain and filled the whole earth" (Dan. 2:35 ESV). Lest we be left scratching our heads over what that stone might be, Daniel gives the interpretation a few verses later:

> In the days of those kings the God of heaven will set up a kingdom that shall never be destroyed, nor shall the kingdom be left to another people. *It shall break in pieces all these kingdoms and bring them to an end, and it shall stand forever,* just as you saw that a stone was cut from a mountain by no human hand, and that it broke in pieces the iron, the bronze, the clay, the silver, and the gold. A great God has made known to the king what shall be after this. The dream is certain, and its interpretation sure. (vv. 44–45 ESV, emphasis added)

These great cities of old—Babylon, Susa, Athens, and Rome—would be struck by a stone. That stone, the kingdom of God, would destroy them in their ancient manifestation and would *replace* them, gathering them up into itself. The principalities are included in the great reconciliation (Col. 1:15–20). Men still gather in cities, and in the case of Athens and Rome, men are still living in the places addressed by this prophecy. But something profound has happened—the City of God is not something far removed from us. The prince of that city is named Immanuel, God *with* us. His name is not God-still-distant or God-removed-from-us.

The kingdom of God does not arrive like the Eighty-second Airborne. The kingdom of God works quietly, inexorably, over the course of many generations.[5] In the new creation, as the Spirit hovers over the face of the nations, just as He hovered over the face of the great deep in the first creation, His presence there precedes any clear indication that His power has been working. But because He is there, His work will be accomplished.

The mountain of the Lord will be established in the earth. All the cities of men will rejoice, as all the families of the earth turn to the Lord. Boston, Istanbul, Dallas, Edinburgh, Berlin, Shanghai, Tehran, Beijing, Seoul, Delhi, Moscow, Tokyo, Mexico City, Santiago, Singapore, Cairo, Mumbai, Lima, Hong Kong, Rio de Janeiro, Baghdad, Bangkok, Bogota, Los Angeles, Jerusalem (of course), Athens, Rome, London, and New York—not one of them will hurt or destroy in all the Lord's holy mountain. The earth will be as full of the knowledge of the Lord as the waters cover the sea, and every city will be a garden city:

> On this mountain the LORD of hosts will make for all
>     peoples
> a feast of rich food, a feast of well-aged wine,
>     of rich food full of marrow, of aged wine well
>         refined.
> And he will swallow up on this mountain
>     the covering that is cast over all peoples,
>     the veil that is spread over all nations.

He will swallow up death forever;
>     and the Lord GOD will wipe away tears from all
>         faces,
>     and the reproach of his people he will take away
>         from all the earth,
>     for the LORD has spoken.
It will be said on that day,
>     "Behold, this is our God; we have waited for him,
>         that he might save us.
This is the LORD; we have waited for him;
>     let us be glad and rejoice in his salvation." (Isa.
>         25:6–9 ESV)

NOTES

INTRODUCTION

1. Jacques Ellul, *The Meaning of the City* (Grand Rapids: Eerdmans, 1970), 8.
2. Dave Hegeman, *Plowing in Hope* (Moscow, ID: Canon Press, 1999), 31.
3. Ellul, *The Meaning of the City*, 5.
4. Carl Sandburg, "Chicago."
5. Peter Leithart, *Against Christianity* (Moscow, ID: Canon Press, 2003), 135.
6. Percy Bysshe Shelley, "Ozymandias."
7. Sir John Glubb, *The Fate of Empires* (London: William Blackwood, 1978), 19.
8. A. N. Wilson, *London: A History* (New York: Modern Library, 2006), 12.
9. Glubb, *The Fate of Empires*, 25.


JERUSALEM

1. "Someone has said that the constant presence of strife is not an interruption of Jerusalem's historical charm—it is Jerusalem's historical charm." George Grant, *Blood of the Moon* (Brentwood, TN: Wolgemuth & Hyatt, 1991), 16.
2. "David's tent was the one and only sanctuary that was built on Zion. 'Zion,' and certainly Zion terminology and symbolism was transferred to the temple mount when Solomon took the ark up to Moriah and set it in the temple, but the original source of the hope of Zion was the tabernacle of David." Peter Leithart, *From Silence to Song* (Moscow, ID: Canon Press, 2003), 73.
3. Barry Fell, *America B.C.: Ancient Settlers in the New World* (Muskogee, OK: Artisan Publishers, 2008).
4. See James B. Jordan, *Darius, Artaxerxes, and Ahasurerus in the Bible.* Studies in Biblical Chronology no. 5 Nicaville, FL: Biblical Horizons, 2001.
5. Flavius Josephus, *The Works of Josephus* (Peabody, MA: Hendrickson Publishers, 1987), 307.
6. Ibid.
7. Abraham Millgram, *A Short History of Jerusalem* (North Bergen, NJ: Aronson, 1998), 26.
8. N. T. Wright, *The Millennium Myth* (Louisville, KY: Westminster John Knox, 1999), 2–3.
9. Millgram, *A Short History of Jerusalem*, xiv.
10. Victor Davis Hanson, *Carnage and Culture* (New York: Doubleday, 2001), 234.
11. Serge Trifkovic, *The Sword of the Prophet* (Boston, MA: Regina Orthodox Press, 2002), 102.
12. Ibid., 97.

13. Ibid., 98.
14. Bernard Lewis, *What Went Wrong?* (Oxford: Oxford University Press, 2002), 3, 7.
15. As quoted in Millgram, *A Short History of Jerusalem*, 132.
16. As quoted in Millgram, *A Short History of Jerusalem*, 139.
17. Melanie Philips, *Londonistan* (New York: Encounter Books, 2006), 152.
19. Trifkovic, *The Sword of the Prophet*, 185.
20. N. T. Wright, *Jesus and the Victory of God* (Minneapolis, MN: Fortress Press, 1996), 126.

ATHENS

1. "Once a year the people had the option (which they did not necessarily take up) of sending a prominent person into exile for a maximum period of ten years." Robin Waterfield, *Athens: From Ancient Ideal to Modern City* (New York: Basic Books, 2004), xix.
2. "The city of Athens prudently kept on hand a number of unfortunate souls, whom it maintained at public expense, for appointed times as well as in certain emergencies." Rene Girard, *Violence and the Sacred* (Baltimore: Johns Hopkins University Press, 1972), 94.
3. "Later the Athenians even had their triremes named *Demokratia, Eleutheria* [Freedom], and *Parrhesia*—nomenclature that would have gotten their captains decapitated in the Persian armada. The idea that a Persian ship would be called *Free Speech* is inconceivable." Hanson, *Carnage and Culture*, 51.
4. Robert Bowie Johnson Jr., *The Parthenon Code* (Annapolis, MD: Solving Light Books, 2004), xi.
5. "Javan is universally identified with the Ionians, or Greeks. The word occurs fairly often in the Old Testament, and is often even translated as 'Greece.'" Henry Morris, *God and the Nations* (Green Forest, AR: Master Books, 2002), 53.
6. "The sheer size of the stonework and the quantity and quality of the gold and silver treasures discovered at Mycenae and elsewhere are evidence of a highly developed and hierarchical society, in which the kings and nobles were given to ostentatious displays of their wealth." Waterfield, *Athens*, 37.
7. Ambrose Bierce, *The Devil's Dictionary* (New York: Dover Publications, 1958), 90.
8. "Zeus' head was split with an axe by Hephaestus (or some other deity, the details varying in different accounts), and the goddess [Athena] sprang out, fully armed and uttering her war cry." *The Oxford Classical Dictionary*, 2d ed. (Oxford: Oxford University Press, 1970), 139.
9. Athena's "most famous cult, that at Athens on the Acropolis, is on the site of a Mycenean palace, the 'house of Erechtheus' of *Odyssey* 7.81." Ibid., 138.

10. Herodotus told of a man by that name being sent to Sparta for help. Centuries later Plutarch told about Eukles, who ran to Athens (in his armor) and announced the victory at Marathon before expiring. Sometime later Lucian of Samosata told Plutarch's story, only with the name of the messenger switched out for the name from Herodotus.

11. "That initial Persian expeditionary force of 490 B.C. was not large by later standards—at most, 30,000 invading troops were pitted against a little more than 10,000 Greeks." Hanson, *Carnage and Culture*, 39.

12. Herodotus, *Histories 6.105*, trans. Robin Waterfield (Oxford: Oxford University Press, 1998), 346.

13. Edward Creasy, *Fifteen Decisive Battles of the World* (New York: Da Capo Press, 1994), 26.

14. Miltiades "led his conquering army by a rapid night-march back across the country to Athens. And when the Persian fleet had doubled the Cape of Sunium and sailed up to the Athenian harbor in the morning, Datis saw arrayed on the heights above the city the troops before whom his men had fled on the previous evening. All hope of further conquest in Europe for the time was abandoned, and the baffled armada returned to the Asiatic coasts." Ibid.

15. "Both Aeschylus and Herodotus, however, were certain that the Persian armada was even larger, numbering more than 1,000 ships and 200,000 seamen. If they are correct, Salamis involved the greatest number of combatants in any one engagement in the entire history of naval warfare." Hanson, *Carnage and Culture*, 43–44.

16. "After the battle the Phoenician admirals came to Xerxes to complain that they had been betrayed by the Ionian Greeks, who had deserted the Persian cause. Their criticism displeased Xerxes, and so he had them all decapitated." Ibid., 51.

17. "When Pythius the Lydian dared to act individually, King Xerxes had his son cut in two." Ibid., 53.

18. Ibid., 54.

19. Lewis Mumford, *The City in History* (New York: MJF Books, 1961), 167.

20. Donald Kagan, *On the Origins of War and the Preservation of Peace* (New York: Doubleday, 1995), 15.

21. Alfred North Whitehead, *Process and Reality* Free Press, 1979 p. 39.

22. "By a metaphysical miracle of the Hellenic will, they appear coupled with each other, and through this coupling eventually generate the art-product, equally Dionysian and Apollonian, of Attic tragedy." Friedrich Nietzsche, *The Birth of Tragedy* (Mineola, NY: Dover Publications, 1995), 1.

23. Acts 17:22–23 ESV.

24. Acts 17:27–28 ESV.

25. "The Greek inheritance, which provided the Western mind with the intellectual basis, at once unstable and highly creative, for what was to

become an extremely dynamic evolution lasting over two and a half millennia." Richard Tarnas, *The Passion of the Western Mind* (New York: Ballantine Books, 1991), 71.

26. "Despite the magnitude of Socrates's influence, little is known with certainty about his life. Socrates himself wrote nothing." Ibid., 31.

27. Ibid., 36.

28. "Western culture is dominated by an approach to knowledge that goes back to Plato, and to his teacher, Socrates. Their love of mathematics and of precise definitions led them to discount any human talent, ability, activity, or skill that could not be defined and explained and subjected to rational argument." Keith Devlin, *Goodbye, Descartes* (New York: John Wiley & Sons, 1997), 182.

29. "Prior to his conversion to Christianity, Justin Martyr (about A.D. 100–163) was a Platonist. After he became a Christian, a number of sub-Christian ideas could still be found in his thought. Origen (A.D. 185–254) believed in the pre-existence of the soul, an obvious residue of Platonism, even after his conversion to Christianity. Even Augustine (A.D. 354–430), the greatest of the church fathers, continued to believe in the preexistence of the soul for several years after his conversion." Ronald Nash, *The Gospel and the Greeks* (Dallas: Probe Books, 1992), 14.

30. "One of the major characteristics of the Hellenistic world was a new kind of cosmopolitanism. More than ever before, the peoples and nations of the Mediterranean world were united. In an even more important sense than mere political union (as under the one government of Rome), they were united by a common law, a common language (Koine Greek) and an increasingly common culture." Ibid.

31. Clifton Fadiman, *The Little, Brown Book of Anecdotes* (Boston: Little, Brown, 1985), 454.

32. "Two of the greatest fourth-century Church Fathers, Basil of Caesarea and his contemporary Gregory of Nazianzus, were educated by pagan orators in Athens. At much the same time and by the same teachers, so was Julian II, 'the Apostate,' the celibate emperor of Rome (360–363), who tried in vain to revive pagan learning and to check the rise of Christianity." Waterfield, *Athens*, 262.

33. The credit goes to "an Athenian-born woman, Aelia Eudokia, whose pagan birth name was Athenais; she was the daughter of a famous Athenian scholar called Leontios. Although it was an arranged marriage [with the emperor Theodosius II] and she converted to Christianity only on the eve of her wedding on 7 June 421, she built one of the earliest churches in Athens, perhaps the earliest." Ibid., 265.

34. "The tenacity of paganism in Athens was due entirely to the presence of the schools, especially Neoplatonism, which offered a viable alternative to Christianity as a way of life and of union with God." Ibid.

35. "Athens was utterly destroyed—not occupied, just destroyed—and this time it was at least two centuries before it began to recover." Ibid.
36. Ibid., 274.
37. "All Europe rallied to the resurrection of Greece. Lord Byron, the very genius of modern Europe, went there. . . . Today, Greece is one nation among others. In the nineteenth century it was much more." Eugen Rosenstock-Huessy, *Out of Revolution* (Oxford: Berg Publishers, 1993 [1938]), 142.
38. Eileen Bigland, *Lord Byron* (London: Cassell & Co., 1956), 48.
39. Acts 20:21; Romans 1:14; 1 Corinthians 1:24; 10:32; 12:13 ESV (emphasis added to all).

ROME

1. "The 'Roman civil wars' were conflicts that afflicted the last century of the Roman republic (88 BC–c. 28 BC) and led to the inevitable institution of the unchallenged authority of one man, the Principate." *The Desk Encyclopedia of World History* (Oxford: Oxford University Press, 2000), 545.
2. "The most striking instance of this morbid and catastrophic decline—and that which most closely resembles our own condition—is that of ancient Rome in the first and second centuries B.C. Here there was no question of senescence. Society came near to dissolution while at the very height of its cultural activity, when its human types were more vigorous than ever before. The danger to civilization came not from the decline of vitality, but from a sudden change of conditions—a material revolution, which broke down the organic constitution of the society." Christopher Dawson, *Dynamics of World History* (Wilmington, DE: ISI Books, 2002), 66–67.
3. "Hannibal Barca ('Grace of Baal Lightning') had little respect for legionary repute. At nine he had sworn an oath of eternal hatred toward Rome." Hanson, *Carnage and Culture*, 110.
4. "After the battle the thirty-one-year-old Hannibal would collect the gold rings of more than eighty consuls, ex-consuls, quaestors, tribunes, and scores of the equestrian class in a bushel." Ibid., 105.
5. "The Colosseum held 45,000 to 50,000 spectators, and to protect them from the fierce summer sun, workers stretched a large canvas canopy over the top." Jack Weatherford, *The History of Money* (New York: Crown, 1997), 47.
6. "Since then each succeeding Emperor has tried to leave some great architectural memorial behind him. Vespasian and Titus have built the Flavian Amphitheater (Colosseum), Trajan a noble Forum, and Hadrian is now completing a magnificent 'Temple of Venus and Rome.'" William Stearns Davis, *A Day in Old Rome* (New York: Allyn and Bacon, 1958), 3.
7. "Rome built the world's first empire organized around money. Whereas the great Egyptian, Persian, and other traditional empires had largely

rejected money in favor of government as the main organizing principle, Rome promoted the use of money and organized all of its affairs around the new commodity." Weatherford, *The History of Money*, 47.

8. "Even during the third and fourth centuries, when the geographical size of the empire declined, the number of soldiers more than doubled from approximately 300,000 to 650,000." Ibid., 51–52.

9. "Then, in 303, he began the horrendous persecution of Christians that was to last for a decade. The persecution of the Christians added money to state coffers and provided plenty of victims for the shows in the Colosseum." Ibid., 59–60.

10. "If the emperor could not obtain much property from the Christians, then he needed to target a wealthier group from whom to confiscate property. Constantine found that wealth in the many well-endowed pagan temples throughout his empire. . . . No matter what his motive, he certainly benefited greatly from the confiscation of temple wealth." Ibid., 60–61.

11. 1 Timothy 2:1–2; 1 Peter 2:17 ESV.

12. "Yet the long and single year now beginning would provide a spectacle of calamity, endurance and survival without parallel, so far, in Rome's history." Kenneth Wellesley, *The Year of the Four Emperors* (London: Routledge, 2000), 1.

13. Josephus, *Antiquities* 18:261–309, trans. William Whiston (Peabody, MA: Hendrickson Publishers, 1987).

14. 2 Thessalonians 2:3–4 ESV.

15. "The date of the birth of Flavius Valerius Constantinus (Constantine the Great), like so much else, is disputed." Michael Grant, *Constantine the Great* (New York: History Book Club, 1993), 15.

16. "Galerius, although Constantine formally sought his recognition, was not at all pleased with this application, but (hiding his resentment no doubt) conceded him the rank of Caesar—granting Severus, however, the superior position in the west, as his own fellow Augustus." Ibid., 23.

17. Maxentius came out of Rome to challenge Constantine because it was the sixth anniversary of his accession, and he was feeling lucky. The second reason "that prompted his departure from Rome, it was asserted, was the fact that the Sibylline Books, which he had consulted, declared that on that day 'the enemy of the Romans would perish.' This advice, which proved, in the end, to mean that Maxentius would be the one to die, was replete with an ambiguity fully worthy of the diplomatic oracular tradition." Ibid., 37.

18. "In 573 Gregory was Prefect of the City, the highest civil dignitary in Rome, president of the Senate with supreme civil jurisdiction within a hundred miles of Rome, in charge of grain supplies, aqueducts, sewers, finance." G. R. Evans, *The Thought of Gregory the Great* (Cambridge: Cambridge University Press, 1986), 4.

19. "Gregory's withdrawal into monastic life was not destined to be permanent. The ascetically inclined ex-prefect was too useful to be left in his monastic retirement." R. A. Markus, *Gregory the Great and His World* (Cambridge: Cambridge University Press, 1997), 10.

20. "That life in general, throughout Europe, became more crude and chaotic, there is little doubt; and that the formative forces were no longer 'Roman' had been true, even before the empire disintegrated. At one moment, the ships bringing papyrus from Egypt would be cut off by pirates; at another, the postal service would go out of existence; or again, an old Roman patrician, on his way to becoming the most important civil officer in Rome, would disappear, and turn up after four years of silence in a Spanish monastery. Famine and disease reduced the population as a whole." Lewis Mumford, *The City in History* (New York: MJF Books, 1961), 248.

21. "To Serenus, bishop of Marseilles, Gregory writes a word of reproach." Evans, *The Thought of Gregory the Great*, 51.

22. "The popes, then, are a major part of the fabric of history. During the last 2,000 years there can be scarcely a place on earth which has not, at some time, felt their touch or found itself changed for better or worse, for a short time or permanently, by their pronouncements, decrees and sometimes personal presence." P. G. Maxwell-Stuart, *Chronicle of the Popes* (London: Thames and Hudson, 1997), 7.

23. R. A. Scotti, *Basilica* (New York: Penguin Group, 2006), 152.

24. In Augustine's view, "Rome . . . had been punished, not replaced." Peter Brown, *Augustine of Hippo* (Berkeley, CA: University of California Press, 1967), 295.

25. Eusebius, *The Church History* (Grand Rapids: Kregel, 1999), 370.

26. Michael Grant, *The History of Rome* (London: Faber and Faber, 1978), 357. Also see Cullen Murphy, *Are We Rome?* (New York: Houghton Mifflin, 2007), 5.

27. "The United States, however, which usually opts for coercive influence rather than annexation, also fits even narrower definitions of empire." Ivan Eland, *The Empire Has No Clothes* (Oakland, CA: Independent Institute, 2004), 23.

28. There is a large and growing discussion about all this, some for and some against. For a sample: "Thus America's is an empire of wealth, an empire of economic success and of the ideas and practices that fostered that success." John Steele Gordon, *An Empire of Wealth* (New York: HarperCollins, 2004), xv. "But America has an amazing ability to not decline. American standards of living surpassed those in Europe around 1740. For about 260 years, in other words, America has been rich and allegedly money-mad and materialistic." David Brooks, *On Paradise Drive* (New York: Simon and Schuster, 2004), 112. "In the past three or

four years, however, a growing number of commentators have begun to use the term *American empire* less pejoratively, if still ambivalently, and in some cases with genuine enthusiasm." Niall Ferguson, *Colossus* (New York: Penguin, 2004), 4. "Though garnished with neologistic flourishes intended to convey a sense of freshness or originality, the politicoeconomic concept to which the United States adheres today has not changed in a century: the familiar quest for an 'open world,' the overriding imperative of commercial integration, confidence that technology endows the United States with a privileged position in that order, and the expectation that American military might will preserve order and enforce the rules. Those policies reflect a single-minded determination to extend and perpetuate American political, economic, and cultural hegemony—usually referred to as 'leadership'—on a global scale." Andrew Bacevich, *American Empire* (Cambridge, MA: Harvard University Press, 2002), 6.

LONDON

1. "Geoffrey of Monmouth, in his *History of the Kings of Britain*, tells how one Brutus, a Trojan warrior, is told by the goddess Diana that 'beyond the setting of the sun, past the realms of Gaul, there lies an island in the sea, once occupied by giants. Now it is empty and ready for your folk. Down the years this will prove an abode suited to you and to your people; and for your descendants it will be a second Troy. A race of kings will be born there from your stock and the round circle of the whole earth will be subject to them.'" Wilson, *London: A History*, 18.

2. "Caesar alleges that some of them lived off meat and milk, and that they dressed in animal-skins; 'and all of them paint their faces with woad (the juice of the *isatis*, a hybrid species) which gives them a blue colouring and makes them seem all the more terrifying in battle. They wear their hair long but otherwise shave, except for the head and upper lip.'" Gerhard Herm, *The Celts* (New York: St. Martin's Press, 1975), 203.

3. "During the eighth and ninth centuries, the terrible Danes came down upon England—first as pirates and ravagers, later to occupy two thirds of the country and eventually to settle down peaceably among people of Anglo-Saxon stock. The Danish tongue being closely related to the Anglo-Saxon (or Old English), the two languages blended in northern England. This fusion simplified the general English tongue, gradually—which became an advantage for the English, long later." Russell Kirk, *America's British Culture* (London: Transaction Publishers, 1993), 15.

4. "Not until King Alfred, late in the ninth century, directed the translation of some important Latin works into the English of the kingdom of Wessex, and commenced the writing of the *Anglo-Saxon Chronicle*, did a written prose literature begin to develop." Ibid.

5. "The Romans started saltworks along the entire east coast. They estab-

lished London in their first year in Britain, and, remembering how Ostia provided for the growth of Rome, they developed saltworks in Essex to provide for what they hoped would become a major port city on the Thames." Mark Kurlansky, *Salt: A World History* (New York: Penguin, 2002), 180. In a fight between the Romans and the native Britons, a Roman general named Suetonius traveled through "'Londinium, a town which, though not dignified by the title of colony, was a busy emporium for traders.' This is the first mention of London in literature. Though fragments of gallic or Italian pottery which may or may not antedate the Roman conquest have been found there, it is certain that the place attained no prominence until the Claudian invaders brought a mass of army contractors and officials to the most convenient bridgehead on the Thames." Winston Churchill, *A History of the English Speaking Peoples: The Birth of Britain* (New York: Barnes & Noble, 1956), 25.

6. The revolt of Boudicea destroyed London. "The slaughter which fell upon London was universal. No one was spared, neither man, woman, nor child. The wrath of the revolt concentrated itself upon all of those of British blood who had lent themselves to the wiles and seductions of the invader. In recent times, with London buildings growing taller and needing deeper foundations, the power-driven excavating machines have encountered at many points the layer of ashes which marks the effacement of London at the hands of the natives of Britain." Churchill, *A History of the English Speaking Peoples*, 26. "The evidence of Boudicea's destruction is to be found in a red level of oxidized iron among a layer of burnt clay, wood and ash. Red is London's colour, a sign of fire and devastation." Peter Ackroyd, *London: The Biography* (New York: Doubleday, 2000), 24.

7. Ackroyd, *London: The Biography*, 209.

8. "We owe London to Rome. The military engineers of Claudius, the bureaucracy which directed the supply of the armies, the merchants who followed in their wake, brought it into a life not yet stilled. Trade followed the development of their road system." Churchill, *A History of the English Speaking Peoples*, 39.

9. "The common law is a body of general rules prescribing social conduct. It applies throughout the realm, save in those special jurisdictions where a recognized local custom or 'liberty' is recognized by the royal courts. The residents of London, for example, kept alive for centuries their own body of peculiar law and custom, confirmed by William the Conqueror, and they were imbued with 'an acute sense of the personality of their city.'" Arthur R. Hogue, *Origins of Common Law* (Indianapolis: Liberty Press, 1966), 188–89.

10. Wilson, *London: A History*, 23.

11. Churchill, *A History of the English Speaking Peoples*,167.

12. Clark Ezra Carr, *Lincoln at Gettysburg* (n.p., 1906), 75.

13. Kirk, *America's British Culture*, 18.
14. David Daniell, ed., *Tyndale's New Testament* (New Haven: Yale University Press, 1989), x.
15. C. S. Lewis, *English Literature in the Sixteenth Century* (Cambridge: Cambridge University Press, 1954), 187.
16. "Never, I believe, were men so little understood and so absurdly maligned as the Puritans." J. C. Ryle, *Light from Old Times* (London: Chas. J. Thynne & Jarvis, 1924), xiv.
17. "In 1560 the most international of all English Bibles appeared, a remarkable result of humanist and Reformation scholarship. English Protestants escaping from Mary had arrived in Geneva, which was then a power-house of textual research and translation into European vernaculars, of secular classics as well as of Scripture. . . . This, the Geneva Bible, was made for readers of all levels, and it was for nearly a century the Bible of the English people, used by all wings of the English church. It was designed to be studied, alone or round the table. It influenced Shakespeare, Milton and very many others." Daniell, ed., *Tyndale's New Testament*, xi.
18. "Henry had broken his kingdom away from its near-millennium of association with the Bishop of Rome, the Pope, head of the Western Christian Church. In a search for cash for the defence of the realm, only fitfully justifying his drastic action in terms of religious reform, he had closed all the religious houses of England, leaving hundreds of monasteries, friaries and nunneries as empty shells to be sold off, torn down by speculative builders, left to rot in remote countryside or converted into country houses for wealthy gentlemen." Diarmaid MacCulloch, *Tudor Church Militant* (London: Allen Lane, 1999), 1.
19. Albert Close, *The Defeat of the Spanish Armada* (East Sussex, UK: Focus Christian Ministries Trust, 1988), 20.
20. Ibid., 39.
21. Lewis, *English Literature in the Sixteenth Century*, 418.
22. For those who want to pursue it, the place to start is Joseph Sobran, *Alias Shakespeare* (New York: Free Press, 1997). Also see Bertram Fields, *Players* (New York: HarperCollins, 2005).
23. Lewis, *English Literature in the Sixteenth Century*, 43.
24. For an outstanding and fresh look at the Puritans, see Leland Ryken, *Worldly Saints* (Grand Rapids: Zondervan, 1986).
25. Charles Grosvenor Osgood, *Poetry as a Means of Grace* (London: Princeton University Press, 1946), 63.
26. It is common for graduates of creative writing workshops to mock Bunyan, but their air of superiority is pathetic. "But this fault is rare in Bunyan—far rarer than in *Piers Plowman*. If such dead wood were removed from *The Pilgrim's Progress* the book would not be very much shorter than it is. The greater part of it is enthralling narrative or genu-

inely dramatic dialogue. Bunyan stands with Malory and Trollope as a master of perfect naturalness in the mimesis of ordinary conversation." C. S. Lewis, *Selected Literary Essays* (Cambridge: Cambridge University Press, 1969), 146. "After the Bible, the book most widely read in seventeenth and eighteenth-century North America was John Bunyan's great Christian allegory *The Pilgrim's Progress* (published in 1678). That fable has been called 'the first English novel'—and, like other major novels, it presents enduring truths in the guise of fiction." Kirk, *America's British Culture*, 22–23.

27. "By a puritan the Elizabethans meant one who wished to abolish episcopacy and remodel the Church of England on the lines which Calvin had laid down for Geneva. The puritan party were not separatists or (in the modern sense) dissenters. . . . There were therefore degrees of puritanism and it is difficult to draw a hard and fast line. . . . By a humanist I mean one who taught, or learned, or at least strongly favoured, Greek and the new kind of Latin; and by humanism, the critical principles and critical outlook which ordinarily went with these studies. Humanism is in fact the first form of classicism. It is evident that if we use the words in this way we shall not see our period in terms of a conflict between humanists and puritans. . . . In reality the puritans and the humanists were quite often the same people." Lewis, *English Literature in the Sixteenth Century*, 18.

28. Lewis, *Selected Literary Essays*, 116.

29. "The Puritans were not enemies to the monarchy. It is simply false to say that they were. The great majority of them protested strongly against the execution of Charles I, and were active agents in bringing back Charles II to England, and placing the crown on his head after Oliver Cromwell's death. The base ingratitude with which they were afterwards treated in 1662, by the very monarch whom they helped to restore, is one of the most shameful pages in the history of the Stuarts." Ryle, *Light from Old Times*, xv–xvi.

30. Philip Benedict, *Christ's Churches Purely Reformed* (New Haven: Yale University Press, 2002), 400. See also William Hetherington, *History of the Westminster Assembly of Divines* (Edmonton: Still Waters Revival Books, 1993), 143.

31. Arthur Herman, *How the Scots Invented the Modern World* (New York: Three Rivers Press, 2002).

32. Wilson, *London: A History*, 39.

33. Ackroyd, *London: The Biography*, 215.

34. "A committee of six was established to direct the rebuilding of the city. One of its members was Christopher Wren who knew already that his idealized version of London was not to be achieved." Ibid., 230–31.

35. Ibid., 232.

36. "God's ways, however, are not as man's ways, and light often arises out of darkness in quarters where it was not expected. At this critical juncture the Nonconformists, to their eternal honour, came forward and cut the knot, and helped the bishops to a right decision. . . . They would have none of the Royal indulgence, if it could only be purchased at the expense of the nation's Protestantism. Baxter, and Bates, and Howe, and the great bulk of the London Nonconformists, entreated the clergy to stand firm, and not to yield one inch to the King." Ryle, *Light from Old Times*, 437–38.

37. "The Killing Time taught Scottish Calvinists to hate governance from London, the Episcopal Church, and Englishmen in general." Herman, *How the Scots Invented the Modern World*, 30.

38. H. A. White as quoted in Morton Smith, *Studies in Southern Presbyterian Theology* (Phillipsburg, NJ: Presbyterian and Reformed Publishing Co., 1962), 18–19. See also Gary DeMar, *America's Christian History: The Untold Story* (Atlanta: American Vision, 1993), and William Dembski, *Never Before in History* (Dallas: Pandas Publications, 1998).

39. George Bancroft, *History of the American Revolution*, 3 vols. (London: Richard Bentley, 1852).

40. And the influence of this enormous number of Scots has been continuing and ongoing. See James Webb, *Born Fighting: How the Scots-Irish Shaped America* (New York: Broadway Books, 2004).

41. Dembski, *Never Before in History*.

42. "But London in 1854 was a Victorian metropolis trying to make do with an Elizabethan public infrastructure. The city was vast even by today's standards, with two and a half million people crammed inside a thirty-mile circumference. But most of the techniques for managing that kind of population density that we now take for granted—recycling centers, public-health departments, safe sewage removal—hadn't been invented yet." Steven Johnson, *The Ghost Map* (New York: Riverhead Books, 2006), 3–4.

43. Ben Wilson, *The Making of Victorian Values* (New York: Penguin, 2007), 26.

44. C. S. Lewis, *The Lion, the Witch and the Wardrobe* (New York: HarperCollins, 1950), 3.

45. Peter Hitchens, *The Abolition of Britain* (New York: Encounter Books, 2002).

NEW YORK

1. Edwin Burrows and Mike Wallace, *Gotham* (Oxford: Oxford University Press, 1999), xiv.

2. "Though no deed of sale exists, the event is generally accepted as having taken place. In a 1626 letter, a Dutch merchant reported he had just

heard, from ship passengers newly disembarked from New Netherland, that representatives of the West India Company had 'purchased the Island Manhattes from the Indians for the value of 60 guilders.' In 1846, using then-current exchange rates, a New York historian converted this figure into twenty-four U.S. dollars. In 1877, another historian asserted (on the basis of no apparent evidence) that the sum had been paid over in 'beads, buttons, and other trinkets.'" Ibid.

3. Jane Mushabac and Angela Wigan, *A Short and Remarkable History of New York City* (New York: Fordham University Press, 1999), 1.

4. Ibid., 3–4.

5. Ibid., 9.

6. Edwin Gaustad, *Liberty of Conscience: Roger Williams in America* (Valley Forge: Judson Press, 1999), 58.

7. Mushabac and Wigan, *A Short and Remarkable History of New York City*, 16–18.

8. Ibid., 17.

9. Gordon, *An Empire of Wealth*, 38.

10. Douglas Kelly, *The Emergence of Liberty in the Modern World* (Phillipsburg, NJ: Presbyterian and Reformed, 1992), 119.

11. Burrows and Wallace, *Gotham*, xii.

12. Creasy, *Fifteen Decisive Battles of the World*.

13. Larry Schweikart and Michael Allen, *A Patriot's History of the United States* (New York: Penguin Group, 2004), 65.

14. For many of the following details, see Richard Ketchum, *Saratoga* (New York: Henry Holt, 1997).

15. Creasy, *Fifteen Decisive Battles of the World*, 304.

16. Marvin Olasky, *Fighting for Liberty and Virtue* (Wheaton, IL: Crossway, 1995), 159.

17. Gordon, *An Empire of Wealth*, 61–62.

18. Ibid.

19. Ibid., 109.

20. Ibid.

21. Ibid., 157–58.

22. Larry Schweikart and Michael Allen, *A Patriot's History of the United States* (New York: Penguin Group, 2004), 155–56.

23. Ibid., 252–53.

24. "Yankee Stadium opens in the Bronx, and thousands of people are turned away for lack of seats. Babe Ruth hits a three-run homer. The Yankees win their first World Series." Mushabac and Wigan, *A Short and Remarkable History of New York City*, 87.

25. Bartlett Giamatti, *A Great and Glorious Game* (Chapel Hill: Algonquin Books, 1998), 46–47.

26. Burrows and Wallace, *Gotham*, 733.

27. Ibid.
28. Giamatti, *A Great and Glorious Game*, 91.
29. Leroy Ashby, *With Amusement for All* (Lexington: University Press of Kentucky, 2006), 96–97.
30. Joseph Schumpter, as quoted in Thomas DiLorenzo, *How Capitalism Saved America* (New York: Crown Forum, 2004), 13.
31. DiLorenzo, *How Capitalism Saved America*, 24.
32. G. Edward Griffin, *The Creature from Jekyll Island: A Second Look at the Federal Reserve* (Westlake Village, CA: American Media, 1994), 64.
33. DiLorenzo, *How Capitalism Saved America*, 44.
34. Mushabac and Wigan, *A Short and Remarkable History of New York City*, 92.
35. Jane Holtz Kay, *Asphalt Nation* (New York: Crown, 1997), 185.
36. Mushabac and Wigan, *A Short and Remarkable History of New York City*, 76.
37. See Lewis, *What Went Wrong?*.
38. Gordon, *An Empire of Wealth*, 38.
39. Weatherford, *The History of Money*, 168–69.
40. Cullen Murphy, *Are We Rome?* (Boston: Houghton Mifflin, 2007), 205–6.
41. Ferguson, *Colossus*, 6.

EPILOGUE

1. As quoted on the frontispiece of Gordon, *An Empire of Wealth*.
2. John Milton, *Areopagitica* (Northbrook, IL: AHM Publishing Corporation, 1951), 50–51.
3. I am indebted for this line of argument to my friend and colleague Peter Leithart, from a sermon he preached at Christ Church in Moscow, Idaho, on Reformation Sunday, 2007.
4. N. T. Wright, *Bringing the Church to the World* (Eugene, OR: Wipf & Stock, 1992), 63.
5. See Douglas Wilson, *Heaven Misplaced* (Moscow, ID: Canon Press, 2008).

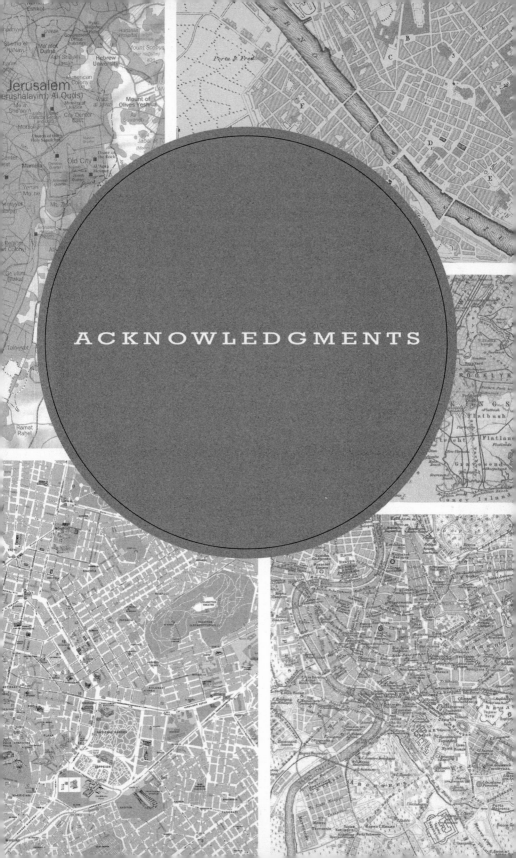

ACKNOWLEDGMENTS

I would like to thank Joel Miller for suggesting this project and my agent Aaron Rench for showing remarkable ingenuity. My family is a constant stay and support—my wife Nancy, my kids and their spouses, and the teeming hordes of grandchildren. And of course, I must also thank Jerusalem, Athens, Rome, London, and New York.

ABOUT THE AUTHOR

Douglas Wilson is a senior fellow of theology at New Saint Andrews College. He has taught both ethics and logic elsewhere at the college level. Editor of Credenda/Agenda, a small cultural journal known for its humorous and satirical flavor, Wilson is also the author of numerous books on education, theology, and culture, including: *The Case for Classical Christian Education*, *Recovering the Lost Tools of Learning*, *Mother Kirk*, and *Angels in the Architecture*, as well as biographies on both Anne Bradstreet and John Knox.

INDEX

# Index

# Index

# Index

Hippias, 54–55
Hitchens, Peter, 150
Holmes, Oliver Wendell (father of the
    Supreme Court justice), 165
Holocaust, 28, 33
Homer, 49–52
Hospital of St. John, 32
Hospitallers, 32
House of Hanover, 143, 144
Howe, William, 160–62
Hudson, Henry, 156
Huguenots, 146
human sacrifice, 46, 90
humanism, 214
Hus, Jan, 124

## I

Iapheti, 47
*Iliad, The* (Homer), 51
immigration (to America), 144–45,
    158–59, 167
incarnation ( of Christ), 187
Independents, 139
Industrial Revolution, 148
*insulae*, 97
Ionians, 47, 54–55, 59, 205, 206
Iraq, 54
Irving, Washington, 159
Isaac (patriarch), 4, 6
Isaiah (the prophet), xxi, 52, 186–87
Islam, xvi, 25–30, 32–33, 178
Israel,
    declared a nation (1948), 35

## J

James I (king), 127, 129, 139, 140, 144
James II (king), 142, 157, 158
Japheth, 47
Jebusites, 3, 5, 6
Jehoshaphat (king of Judah), 9
Jephthah (judge in ancient Israel), 52
Jeroboam (king), 10
Jerome, 106

Jerusalem, 1–41
    crusader period, 28–33
    felling by Muslim conquerors, 26
    felling by Rome, 24
    Muslim era, 25–28
    origin of name, 5
Jesus, 21–23, 39–41, 80, 99, 105, 186–87,
    192–93, 197–98
jihad, 27
John of Gaunt, 124, 125
John Paul II (pope), 111
Johnson, Robert Bowie, 47
Jonson, Ben, 135
Josephus, 13, 16, 17
Judah (tribe), 11
judges, period of (Israel), 6, 7, 9–10
Julian the Apostate, 74, 207
Julius Caesar, 89, 93–94, 120
Juno (Gr. Hera), 86–87
Justin Martyr, 72, 206

## K

Kagan, Donald, 60–61
Kay, Jane Holtz, 176
King James Version (of the Bible), 127,
    129
Kipling, Rudyard, 185
Kirk, Russell, 126, 211–12
Knickerbocker Base Ball Club, 168
Knights of Malta, 32
Knights Templar, 31
Knox, John, 131
Koran, 27, 178

## L

Latimer, Hugh (bishop of Worcester),
    131
Latinus, 86
League of Nations, 34, 38
Leithart, Peter, xvii, 218
Lenapes, 156
Lepanto, battle of, 26, 28, 33
Leo IV, 75

# Index

# Index

# Index

# Index